ESSAYS IN ACCOUNTING THOUGHT:

ESSAYS IN ACCOUNTING THOUGHT

A Tribute to W. T. Baxter

edited by

Irvine Lapsley

Edinburgh, The Institute of
Chartered Accountants of Scotland, 1990

CONTENTS

ACKNOWLEDGEMENTS

It would not have been possible to produce this book without the generous contributions from very busy people. The fact that they have chosen to give of their time in this way is a mark of the respect in which W.T. Baxter is held. Professor Baxter also kindly agreed to the inclusion of his inaugural lecture, 'Accounting as Academic Study', in a 'collection of papers' which I was seeking to publish. Apologies for not being more explicit, Will, but I hope that you are happy with the result. This paper was published originally in 'The Accountant' and Lafferty Publications have also agreed to its inclusion in this book. The publication of this book was supported by a grant from the Scottish Chartered Accountants' Trust for Education and a bequest from the late Sir William Slimmings and this is gratefully acknowledged. The idea of the book was encouraged by Ian Marrian of the Institute of Chartered Accountants of Scotland. Christine Waugh of the Institute was extremely helpful in the production of the book. Last, but not least, my secretary, Audrey Smith gave her usual patient and generous spirit in compiling this book.

Irvine Lapsley
Edinburgh
July, 1996

The Institute of Chartered Accountants of Scotland wholly supports Irvine Lapsley's initiative in bringing together these essays from friends and colleagues.

CONTRIBUTORS

William T. Baxter
Professor Emeritus, London School of Economics

Michael Bromwich
CIMA Professor of Accounting and Financial Management, London School of Economics

Sir Bryan Carsberg
Secretary-General, International Accounting Standards Committee

John Flower
Director, Centre for Research in European Accounting

John Forker
Professor of Accounting, Queen's University, Belfast

Joanne Horton
Lecturer in Accounting, Bristol University

Anthony Hopwood
Professor of Management Studies, Oxford University and President, EIASM

Irvine Lapsley
Professor of Accounting, University of Edinburgh

Richard Macve
Professor of Accounting, London School of Economics

John Perrin
Honorary Fellow, Exeter University and Professor Emeritus, Warwick University

Sir John Shaw
Deputy Governor, Bank of Scotland and Visiting Professor, University of Glasgow

Sir David Tweedie
Chairman, Accounting Standards Board

Geoffrey Whittington
Price Waterhouse Professor of Financial Accounting, University of Cambridge

PREFACE to
"Essays in Honour of Will Baxter"

It is a signal honour to be invited to contribute this preface to a book honouring Will Baxter's 90th birthday.

Will Baxter's early years followed the path of a conventional Edinburgh childhood and entry into professional life: education at George Watson's College and the University of Edinburgh was followed by training to qualify as a Chartered Accountant in the archetypal small partnership of Scott, Moncrieff, and then moving on qualification to Graham, Smart and Annan. Annan then held the Chair of Accounting and Business Method as a part-time appointment and provided an early opportunity for the bright young Baxter to engage in academic work on his return from study at Harvard as a Commonwealth Fund Fellow. (Will subsequently described that part-time assistant lectureship - which carried a stipend of £300 - as "the lowest of the low").

That does not seem the characteristic background for a revolutionary. But Will Baxter, despite - or is it because of - his personal gentleness, has been one of accountancy's most influential revolutionaries. He himself has explained how his revolutionary passion evolved.

During the 1930's he met and became friendly with a number of the young British and American economists then interesting themselves in the interface between accounting and economics. The traditional accountant's search for accuracy in financial measurement was driven by his origins in the Law in helping to define in financial terms the extent of competing claims on business assets. Distinctions between "capital" and "revenue", between the Balance Sheet and the Income Statement, were fundamental. For the economist the concepts of "value" and "income" are directly inter-related. The conflict inherent in these two views of measuring and assessing the impact of commercial cash flows was made explicit by those friends and collaborators of Will Baxter.

He has described how he initially found their ideas shocking, and how disturbed he was by their vigorous intellectual challenges to his early certainties, built as they were on a confident mastery of the techniques of book-keeping and on a sound grounding in the principles of the law.

In retrospect, it is a pity that the early lead of the Scottish Universities in establishing accountancy as an academic discipline did not provide there the opportunity to explore productively the expansion of the subject's early frontiers. Perhaps that was precisely because so many of those early University appointments were part-time - as were Annan's and Baxter's own. Busy practitioners preoccupied with the practical problems of their clients were perhaps not best-placed to participate vigorously in challenging debate, which at the very least questioned most of the assumptions on which their fee-earning work was based!

In the event, having determined on an academic career, Will Baxter had to look abroad to the University of Cape Town for his first professorial appointment, in 1937. Then he found an environment not dissimilar from the Scottish tradition of explaining to aspirant practitioners the practical principles underlying the detailed procedures of their profession. But he kept in close touch with his many friends on both sides of the Atlantic, and continued to develop his thinking and writing from the standpoint of thoughtful criticism.

In 1947 he "came home" to the London School of Economics where as Professor of Accounting for 26 years he contributed vigorously to teaching, research, and to the development of his chosen discipline. Since leaving that post the most recent two decades of his life have been marked by a continuing flow of elegantly expressed, tightly argued, and challenging views on the issues which preoccupy accountants, those who use accounts, and those with responsibility for formulating business policy. He has interested himself, and illuminated the thinking of others, on such topics as goodwill, depreciation, replacement cost and deprival value accounting, accounting standards, and the objectives and usefulness of accounting research.

Will Baxter has been a tireless advocate of the need for relevance in research, which means for him that the studies and analyses of academics will be of help in professional and business offices. And he has always expressed the hope that the practitioner and the standard setter would seek the help of the academic in defining a framework of accounting principles to lead towards better accounts. These are not views which are necessarily popular either with academics or with practitioners. One suspects that from time to time Will Baxter has sighed regretfully at observing all that still remains to be done to bring these two strands fruitfully together.

Academic honours have been heaped on Professor Emeritus William Threipland Baxter, D.Litt, B.Com, CA. They include Honorary Fellowship of both the London School of Economics, where he achieved so much, and of the University of Edinburgh, where he began. All the many distinctions he has earned will have brought him pleasure. I share with others who have written at greater length in this book the hope that this tribute to his many achievements will also please him. Here is a man who is able to command affection, admiration and respect, and who has influenced and informed the work of generations of students, researchers and practitioners.

WILL BAXTER - GENTLE REVOLUTIONARY

Irvine Lapsley

This book tries to trace some of the influences which W.T. ('Will') Baxter has brought to bear upon accounting thought and practice. To this end, we have a collection of papers in this book which seek to capture the key elements of 'the Baxter contribution' - thoughts from the world of practice (Sir David Tweedie and Sir Bryan Carsberg) on which he placed great value, although often in a critical fashion, the issue of standardisation and related financial reporting problems (Geoffrey Whittington, John Perrin, John Forker, Joanne Horton and Richard Macve), the particular influence of management accounting on Will Baxter's thinking (Michael Bromwich), John Flower's assessment of "accounting heros" from continental Europe, to place Will Baxter's contribution in a wider perspective and, finally, Anthony Hopwood's essay which takes up Will Baxter's critical perspective on the direction of accounting research, and his desire for inter-disciplinary research.

As part of this process of tracing the Baxter influences this short paper moves from the public domain of academic writings to Will Baxter, the person. It may seem strange that an academic at the University of Edinburgh should edit a collection of papers in honour of Professor Emeritus, W.T.Baxter, of the LSE, on the occasion of his 90th birthday and reflect on Will Baxter, the person. But there are connections, even if these are not immediately obvious. At one level there is the formal connection -W.T.Baxter was the first lecturer (see S.P.Walker, 1994) in accounting at this university - but this was in the 1930s, before I was born. There are other connections - we are both members of the Institute of Chartered Accountants of Scotland and W.T.Baxter has acknowledged the influence of the world of accounting practice on his research and this also influenced me (my preoccupation is with the public sector and I still remember being puzzled, as a CA apprentice, at why local authority accounts had to be so different from any others which I encountered). In academic life the ebb and flow of ideas are more complex than the above connections can depict and this short tribute to 'Will Baxter is a story about how his thinking has influenced me, in an attempt to show, more generally, why Professor Baxter is not only held in the highest regard, but is also someone for whom there is a great store of affection in the academic world and in practice.

The Beginning

It was May 1969. There had been a year of revolution, of students taking to the streets challenging the governments of the day. A year when revolutionary student leaders, such as Daniel Cohn-Bendit had made leading radical thinkers, such as Herbert Marcuse, look like establishment figures of the day. A year of student sit-ins and demonstrations. The professor strode in to the lecture theatre. He was tall. Imposing. His impatience with the establishment was evident in his lectures - always questioning, probing the raison d'être of the status quo. In his own way, a revolutionary figure. Professor Stamp was not a man to be meddled with. The late Edward (known affectionately as 'Eddie' by many, including his students, but we would never have dared to say this, if he was in earshot) Stamp, Professor of Accountancy at Edinburgh University, was about to speak. We listened intently. He had invited a guest lecturer to address us - a Professor Baxter from LSE. My memory does not hold the exact words Edward Stamp used, but I do recollect his reverence (most unusual from our hard-hitting, critical professor), and his tribute to Professor Baxter's contribution to advancing accounting thought, as he encouraged us to hear what the professor from LSE had to say. Come the day, Professor Baxter addressed us. To my mind there was a clear correspondence between this professor's ideas and those of Edward Stamp. But this man from LSE was simultaneously provocative, yet benign and kind - a **gentle** revolutionary.

Second Phase

Professor Baxter is on record as stressing the importance of collegial environment in the development of ideas. Richard Brief edits a distinguished series of books on accounting history, one of which, W.T.Baxter, <u>Accounting Theory</u>, was published, this year. In his introduction to this book, Professor Baxter tells the story of the beginning of his academic career at Edinburgh University in which he shared a room with Kenneth Boulding, the distinguished economist, who was then at the start of his career, too. This was in the 1930s, and Will Baxter acknowledges this, as the start of economics influencing his own thinking.

In 1974, forty years after the young Will Baxter and Ken Boulding had engaged in debate as young academics at this university, John Forker and I were appointed to lectureships at Edinburgh university. (John Forker will be embarrassed profoundly at the construction of a sentence in which our names appear with those of Baxter and Boulding, but this is merely to draw the parallel that the discussions of young academics in their formative years are extremely influential). John Forker was a qualified accountant, with a first degree in economics and a master's degree in accounting and finance from LSE. This was one of the happiest periods of my academic career. John Forker introduced me to Baxter's ideas of deprival value and we used to debate this, continually, from a variety of perspectives - was it possible to achieve meaningful accounting values, could we think of situations where the decision rule of "value to the business" might break down, how did this sit with the decision relevance models being used to construct a conceptual framework for financial reporting. During our extended discussions, it became evident that John Forker was a great admirer of Professor Baxter - not only his ideas but also his clarity of exposition, his dedication as a scholar. And, through John Forker, I came to share that admiration of W.T.Baxter's work.

Main Stage

In 1976, John Perrin, a graduate of LSE, where he completed his Ph.D studies in the 1950s was about to undertake research into public sector capital accounting at Warwick University, and was seeking two research fellows to assist him in this task. It was my good fortune that John Perrin saw fit to appoint me to one of these posts. There were two particular strands to this research project which benefited from Baxter's vision of accounting. The issue of deprival value was a matter which we addressed as part of this study. But there was also a preoccupation with what Will Baxter has called the impact of accounting research on 'the office', or the world of practice (W.T.Baxter, 1988). In John Perrin's view (which I share still) there was (and still is) a need to go inside organisations to study accounting practices. This was a fundamental aspect of the Warwick research led by John Perrin.

As part of that research project, John Perrin had established an advisory committee which consisted of leading practitioners of the day, an economist (Professor Reddaway from Cambridge) and an accountant (Professor Baxter). In discussions with John Perrin it was evident that he shared John Forker's admiration for W.T.Baxter, both as an academic and as a 'real gentleman'. And so it was that I first met W.T.Baxter. He was kind, gentle and courteous. The format of these meetings was that we presented ideas or findings and members of the committee would respond. The other research fellow was an extremely able economist (A.J.Owen) and he faced the razor sharp questions of Professor Reddaway. Meanwhile I was biding my turn to face Professor Baxter, but I could see how kind and gentle he looked and had my extensive exchanges with John Forker not prepared me for anything he could throw at me? Well, no. That was when I discovered Will Baxter was capable of asking the most penetrating of questions. I should add that, at that time, the department of accounting at Edinburgh was noted for its distinctive, 'pro-cash flow, allocation-free' accounting. After engaging with Will Baxter and John Perrin my initial hostility to capital asset accounting, particularly in the NHS, changed. I returned to Edinburgh as the departmental heretic.

On the Circuit

Academic conferences are superb for meeting new people and ideas, where papers can be tested out before critical audiences before appearing in print. This is the ideal venue for bright young academics to keep abreast of the latest ideas in their subject area. And this is where I next encountered Will Baxter -by then long retired, but still enjoying academic debate. Will said he remembered me when I introduced myself (too polite to say otherwise). On these occasions I found another aspect of Will Baxter - a wicked sense of humour. In Venice, at the annual congress of the European Accounting Association, he remarked to me that "it was good to see that young Whittington was still active". This made me chuckle and I think that he knew it would. Just like the annual congress of the EAA in Turku, in Finland, when he told me that he was learning Finnish (a fiendishly difficult language, I know from my own inadequate attempts at French, German and Italian) in his spare-time and what was I doing in my spare-time?

4

Completing the Picture

Events in the 1990s presented a more complete picture of Will Baxter. The 75th anniversary of the study of accounting at Edinburgh University was in 1994. To celebrate this event, Falconer Mitchell (our head of department), Stephen Walker (a Scottish CA, but also a first rate archival researcher) and myself put our minds to these celebrations. Stephen Walker faced the task of writing a book on the department's history with extremely sketchy departmental records, but his training as an archival researcher stood him in good stead as he sought out other records within the university and at the Institute of Chartered Accountants of Scotland. This documented the appointment of W.T.Baxter to the first lectureship in accounting at Edinburgh University - previously all appointments had been professors (part-time).

Falconer Mitchell delegated me with the task of contacting Will Baxter to see if he would join us in our celebrations. Not only did he agree, readily, but he also said that he would be delighted to present a paper. On the day of our conference Will Baxter was scheduled to speak first and I was in the chair. With the assistance of his wife we checked out the acoustics of the lecture theatre, with Will wearing a small microphone which I pinned to his lapel. At this point, there were no lecture notes in sight and I felt a little apprehensive, I introduced Professor Baxter, and he leapt to the podium, before I could pin the microphone to his lapel - and still no sign of any notes for his speech! My apprehension increased, but, needlessly, as Will Baxter's speech was clear, lucid, critical with a fair sprinkling of humour. Members of the audience who had heard Will Baxter's lectures at LSE in their student days assured me that this was how he was then and he never had notes. That presentation was not included in the book of readings published from that conference (Will Baxter had other plans for it), but he did contribute another piece which he had been working on, on asset valuation (Baxter, 1996), which he considered suitable for publication only after he had made sufficient revisions to tighten his argument.

Will Baxter - Gentle Revolutionary

Sir John ('Jack') Shaw has hinted at Will Baxter's gentle nature as a great strength in the preface to this book. This short piece has sought to reaffirm that perspective. It is highly probable that others more closely associated with Will Baxter could have written a better piece. It is also certain that, in compiling this collection of essays, I have inadvertently omitted potential contributions from persons well able and suited to do so (as I write this I shudder as I recollect one of our most senior academics, who is not a contributor, telling me of a discussion with Will Baxter which was instrumental in him pursuing an academic career rather than a career in practice), and I can only ask the forgiveness of people so slighted and that they join in the spirit of this book ... and wish Will Baxter all the best on his 90th birthday.

References

Baxter, W.T. (1988) <u>Accounting Research: Academic Trends versus Practical Needs</u>, ICAS, 1988.

Baxter, W.T. (1996) <u>Accounting Theory</u>, Garland Publishing, 1996.

Baxter, W.T. (1996) "Assets' Versus Firm's Value: What if the Parts Exceed the Whole?", pp.35-39, in I.Lapsley & F.Mitchell, <u>Accounting and Performance Measurement: Issues in the Private and Public Sectors</u>, Paul Chapman, 1996.

Walker, S.P. (1994) <u>Accountancy at the University of Edinburgh, 1919-1994: The Emergence of a 'Viable Academic Department</u>, ICAS, 1994.

ACCOUNTING AS AN ACADEMIC STUDY[1]

W.T.Baxter

It is fitting that a new professor should be made to defend his subject, and doubly so when his subject is new too. We should always look cautiously at thin ends of wedges. Further, the custom gives a slightly sporting flavour to inaugural lectures; there is always just a chance that the raw professor may fail to make out a case for his subject, and so may feel forced to end his address by handing in his resignation. Unfortunately, academic history does not tell us of many cases in which this has happened.

While accounting managed to win its way into some British universities several decades since, its place has so far been small and uncertain. Mine is, I think, the first full-time chair to be created in Britain; and many universities are only this year appointing their first full-time - or even part-time - instructors. So a heavy responsibility lies on this tiny group of teachers. What are we going to make of our new subject? Accounting, as practised, may well include many things both interesting and useful; but can we select from and arrange these things in such a way as to build as stiff academic discipline? Can accounting contribute something to a student's mental training that will be worth having even if, after graduating, he never again sets eyes on a balance sheet?

In part from lack of courage, in part from lack of time, I propose to evade the fundamental question of whether a university should have any truck at all with professional subjects. These have for centuries been forcing their way into the syllabus. Sometimes the gate-crasher has ended as an honoured guest; latin was, I fancy, at first taught largely in order that professional men might earn their bread and butter. But this is far from meaning that every professional subject has an automatic right to a place. Nor would I suggest that such subjects ought not to be balanced by work in very different fields if we are to give a liberal education. Techniques, sciences, even languages do not

provide a sufficient educational background for citizens of a free nation. For such a programme lacks contact with both man's emotional experience as an individual and his practical experience as a gregarious animal. ... Unless the educational process includes at each level of maturity some continuing contact with those fields in which value judgements are of prime importance, it must fall far short of the ideal. The student in high school, in college, and in graduate school must be concerned, in part at least, with the words "right" and "wrong" in both the ethical and the mathematical sense. Unless, he feels the import of those general ideas and aspirations which have been a deep moving force in the lives of men, he runs the risk of partial blindness." (J.B.Conant, in Harvard University, President's Report (1946), p.9.)

Accounting Blends Several Subjects

The nature of accounting is such that its teacher is in the happy position of being able to range far and wide over everything related to financial administration. For the most remarkable thing about accounting as a field of study is that it is not so much a subject by itself as a synthesis of other subjects. The sole original contribution of accounting - narrowly defined - to man's mental store-cupboard is double-entry book-keeping. If, as I believe to be the case, accountants have built up a not unimpressive fabric of practice, they have done so by their skill in adapting, and perhaps improving on, what has been learnt in other spheres, notably the law and commerce. The role of double-entry is to fuse together the different elements into one amalgam; and this it does neatly and well. Perhaps some genius may eventually hit on a better basis for keeping records, but such a system is hard to imagine. The first aim of the serious student of accounting must then be to master double-entry.

The task is not easy, and all too often it is long and dull into the bargain (though I do not concede the dullness to be inevitable). Therefore it seems a thousand pities that the syllabus of most schools, and even of higher institutions, never gets beyond the double-entry stage. One would feel sorry for the student of a language who did not pass from the memorising of conjugations to the delights of the new literature; in the same way, a short course in accounting is apt to be all pill, no jam. It is therefore natural for a university to ask whether there is no method of side-stepping this first stage -no by-pass to the advanced studies that are, after all, what the business administrator will be mainly concerned with.

The answer is that such an approach is perfectly feasible, and in some cases may be justified. Your budding director would get great help from a short course of lectures in which, say, general finance is explained with the aid of balance sheets, and trends are analysed with consecutive profit and loss

8

accounts. Such an outline may cover his likely minimum needs, and will certainly be immensely more useful to him at the board-room table than a smattering of beginner's book-keeping alone. Indeed, one could argue that too much familiarity with double-entry may in some ways be a handicap. Thus there was an unpardonable delay before companies took to publishing accounts in a form that was likely to be intelligible to their average shareholder; to-day, some companies still pay scant attention to this duty, and even their more scrupulous neighbours tend to show little imagination or taste for experiment. The reason is probably that the men responsible cannot shake themselves free from the technicalities of double-entry; forgetting how innocent of book-keeping are their readers, they frame accounts that are crude reflections of the debit and credit skeleton rather than attempts to interest and inform.

I have tried in the preceding paragraph to make out the strongest possible case for a short-cut training that skips drill in double-entry and deals only in principles. But I must confess that I have failed to persuade myself. Such a training is apt to be pretentious and even dangerous. It can, I think, be justified only when extreme pressure on time rules out anything more thorough. All figures for costs, values, and the like are full of pitfalls. They are profoundly influenced by the machinery that gathers them; unless the manager of a business has the feel of this machinery in his very bones, he will frequently be misled, and will always be at the mercy of his subordinates.

An analogy may make my attitude plainer. The lover of music may enjoy concerts without having learnt ot play a note; and his enjoyment may well be increased by listening to talks on the instruments of the orchestra or the lives of the great composers - with no drudgery at five-finger exercises. But one scarcely supposes that such a training will produce many first-class critics, still less composers or performers.

Because of this need for a preliminary training, I question whether a short course in book-keeping and accounting is worth putting into a university's commerce syllabus. Students whose main aim is not to become managers of business (e.g. engineers) may be none the worse for a superficial survey; but with commerce students it is surely a case of all or nothing. Unless the subject is taken for, say, two years (so that a grounding in double-entry can be followed by an introduction to the higher flights), the student can probably use his time better in other class-rooms and will be spared the dangers of a little learning.

The Influence of Business Organisation

One important factor in determining whether or not a subject is worth a place in a scheme of education is the degree to which it demands prolonged attention to a core of principles. It makes good food when it gives the student something that he can chew on for a long time. All too often, alas, accounting is presented as a series of disconnected fragments, without any underlying theme except double-entry, and governed by isolated and arbitrary rules rather than sustained reasoning.

Even in the elementary stages, when the beginner still flounders in double-entry, his work can be lightened and given point if he is taught to view book-keeping as the handmaid of the business manager. As each new problem is introduced, the sequence of reasoning should be, first, 'What does a business man want to know about this?' and, next, 'How then should the facts be dealt with by the book-keeper?' Our students should also be shown that the accountant's task is not only to record, but to plan a business in such a way as to stop error and fraud. In other words, the lecturer ought to discuss the procedures that we name 'internal check'. Strong reasons prompt the young administrator to learn this subject thoroughly. Excellent mental training is given by study of the principles of embezzlement; for here success demands mastery of the whole financial structure in all its ramifications, and a crystal-clear insight into the remotest effects of any transaction. If he comes to the counting-house armed with a knowledge of internal check, the administrator can make fraud next to impossible; what is more he will be able to save expense and work by bringing in short-cuts. Thus he may at once increase his profits and spare his staff from drudgery and temptation. Seldom do self-interest and humanity lie so close together.

But businesses are not isolated. They have dealings with the outside world. So, if the first strand in accounting is internal management, the next is law. Much of accounting might be called legal arithmetic.

Historically, indeed, it was probably this strand that came first; the most pressing reason for keeping accounts is to remember what you owe and are owed. At a slightly later stage in business history, a wish to record the legal rights of partners in their joint wealth gave another push to book-keeping. I quote from the earliest accounting text-book in English:

'negligence of kepyng bokes hath caused more striefe in lawe and variance of children and frendes than any one thyng in the world; seruantes and factors haue vndone their Masters, riche men hath sodenly become beggers and could not tell how it should come to passe ...'

The writer warns us of the troubles that plague executors if the dead man kept no accounts

'whiche leueth to the world all thynges rawly and vnperfectly, and causeth some in the place of "God haue mercie on his solle" to saie the devill gnaw the bones of hym, and a vengeance on suche a keeper of a boke'.

These early needs were, however, child's play compared with what has come since. An accountant must now be at home with the law of companies, of bankruptcy, of executors and - above all - of taxation. A university training in accounting must accordingly have a heavy bias towards law. This is by no means a matter of regret. For the law - rightly taught - is a discipline that blends well with accounting. Especially among the older generation of accountants, one often sees the happy results of the union - in a keeper and surer grasp, not merely of the legal aspects, but of all other branches of our subject.

I think that this is a particularly appropriate place at which to pay tribute to my predecessor, the late Mr S W Rowland. For he was an obvious case of an accountant whose abilities had been quickened by a legal training. His lectures and his many articles in the accounting press had a strong legal flavour; and his books are enriched with illustrations from case law, and are specially useful in showing how book-keeping reflects legal relationships. It is a matter of keep regret to me that Mr Rowland's sudden death has robbed me of his friendship and guidance.

The Influence of Economics

I have tried to show that the teacher of accounting needs to work hand-in-glove with his fellows in the departments of commerce and law. A third contribution to his task could come from economics. The lack of any liaison between accounting and economic theory is so marked and so astonishing as to call for a whole lecture to itself. Each subject has grown up in serene indifference to the other, although both try to solve much the same problems, and in certain places the degrees of overlapping is remarkable.

Some of these common topics occur readily to the mind; the theory of costs and of revenue are cases in point. Less obvious, but perhaps of more importance, is valuation. If the teacher of accounting is seeking a backbone for his lectures, I suggest that valuation supplies it to a surprising degree. For, if an accountant is worth his salt, he will not be content merely to know how to insert given figures into his records; he ought also to have ideas on what these figures should be. And almost all the less simple business transactions involve valuation.

Valuation Theory

His text-books warn the young accountant that he is no valuer, and doubtless this is true enough so far as single physical objects go. But he may be called on to value less tangible things. Examples are:

(1)   *Shares.* Where a company's shares are not quoted on the Stock Exchange, they must sometimes be valued artificially. An accountant may be called upon to make the appraisal - either because he is the company's auditor, or simply because he is deemed to be knowledgeable in such matters.

(2)   *Partnership rights.* Almost all the problems of partnership hinge on valuation. When a new partner is to be admitted, the existing partners will naturally form some idea of what his admission will mean to them in terms of increased gains to the firm, less his share of the gains.

For his part, he will doubtless compare the benefits of partnership with his prospects elsewhere. Some of the factors can scarcely be appraised in terms of money, for they include prestige, friendship, and loss of freedom; here, as in the partnership of marriage, it is perhaps just as well that most men are not given to weighing the endless pros and cons too nicely or a decision might never be reached.

Again, when a partner dies or retires, he is presumably entitled to withdraw some of the wealth that he has helped to create. But how much? Logic may suggest that he or his heirs should receive the capitalised value of:

(a)   what the remaining partners will earn without him; less

(b)   what they would have earned had he stayed in the firm.

But here a clash arises between the ideal and the expedient. Such a concept may gratify logic, but it does not lend itself readily to conversion into a crisp and final sum of £sd. It involves guesswork about future prospects; if his payment depended on such a highly subjective estimate, the retiring man might well be startled to discover how weak was the faith of his partners - who have to foot the bill - in the firm's future. He would find it hard to coax them round to his own cheerful views; his widow and orphans would find it even harder. Plainly then, some rule that is objective, and leaves scant scope for bickering, is a much better means for determining his compensation than one that is right in theory - or even equity - but which hinges on personal feeling.

(3)   *A whole business.* When a business is bought, expropriated, appraised for death duties, or amalgamated with another business, accountants may be asked to suggest a value. Here, again, the question arises of whether the answer is to be found by speculating about future earnings or looking backwards at past results. The latter process, with its seeming certainty and objectivity, is the more tempting; but the answer so found is apt to be brushed aside

contemptuously when buyers and sellers come to grips. Here we are not trying to deal justly with a widow or orphans, but to recreate the conditions of the real market. The latter seems to look forward, not back. However unsubstantial and controversial may be our guesses about the future, they are the stuff that prices are made of. The accountant is therefore forced willy-nilly to don the prophet's mantle if he becomes a valuer.

He is at once confronted with two more problems. First, to what extent can he use old data as guides to future earnings? Common sense suggests that there is normally some continuity between the past and the future - that to-day is a link rather than a barrier between yesterday and to-morrow - and that accordingly profits are likely to follow a trend. Secondly, what is the relationship between future earnings of the whole business and the present market values of its separate assets? If the value of the business is a function solely of future income, does this mean that we can shut our eyes to the individual assets? I think not; but a clear exposition of the relation between these two aspects of wealth has yet to be made. Much is being said about the need for accounting research. I can imagine no more useful field than this.

Capital and Revenue

We pass almost imperceptibly from the string of problems that have valuation as their common theme to those that find unity in the need to measure capital and revenue. For is not revenue a growth in value? There is, I know, a strong school of thought among accountants that does not altogether accept this view. It prefers the profit and loss account to the balance sheet as the basis of approach, that is, it deems net revenue to be the difference between incomes and costs rather than a 'value accretion'. But can incomes and costs be divorced from value? 'Income' is surely something that has been gained; and 'cost' seems to imply that something has been sacrificed. Now, what are these somethings if they are not changes in the value of wealth? It is hard to conceive of water flowing into or out of a tank without altering the quantity in the tank. Similarly, I cannot understand incomes and costs that do not effect the value of the net assets.

14

In any case, nobody denies that we must pay heed to the values of at least some assets, such as stocks, before we can find profit. So, whichever approach we favour, we cannot shirk this issue of valuation entirely. It raises intriguing problems. For instance, how should a manufacturer value his work in progress, and what figure should a building contractor place upon unfinished structure? How should we measure the depreciation of a wasting asset? I must humbly confess that I do not know of any adequate answers. Many have been suggested in writings on accounting; all fail to satisfy. The reason is, I think, that they deal with different assets piecemeal, without first trying to give a general definition. Reason will never be content with rules for valuing each specific asset unless they harmonise with an overall principle. The first thing that we must do, then, is to produce our fundamental definitions of capital and revenue. Till we have such definitions, we can only agree with the sad comment on present-day practice:

> 'What is set out as a measure of net income can never be supposed to be a fact in any sense at all except that it is the figure that results when the accountant has finished applying the procedure which he adopts.'

Here, surely, is another problem beckoning to the would-be researcher. I must, however, warn him of two important but somewhat contradictory needs. First, as I have just said, his only hope of creating a satisfactory body of rules is to start by finding a basic principle. Second, his principle and rules are not likely to be of much use unless they can be fitted into current practice without too harsh a shock. He may indeed tell us to mend our ways within reason; few of us would deny that there is room for improvement. But his hope must be to perceive, thanks to a freshness of insight, some germ in existing practice that can be fairly easily developed and extended to cover all cases.

It may sound confused to plead for a profound new principle in one paragraph and to give conservative warnings in the next. Let me try to clear up the muddle. One can conceive of a vast range of definitions of revenue, all of which would be thoroughly pleasing to the mind. The differences between them would lie in the *time* at which approaching gains are deemed to have reached us; what sign shall we require to prove that the bird in the bush has become the bird in the hand? I doubt whether any answer to this question can be found in detached thought. In other words, when we are faced with the job of turning a revenue concept into definite figures, we are apt to get bogged among many rival definitions, none of which seems capable of proving its superiority on abstract grounds. We must therefore test the definitions in the light of their usefulness. Why does a business man want to know his income? Various answers come to mind - for instance, to measure efficiency, to see how his investment is paying, to find what surplus should be shared among the joint owners (including that ever-present though invisible partner, the Chancellor). Probably the best definition of revenue is the one that yields the best answer to these questions. Important corollaries are that the answer must not cost too much to find, that it will be understood by as many people as possible, and that it will not leave endless room for squabbling. This can mean only that our basic principle must not be too alien to existing notions.

Cost

The theory of cost is another topic that may well be used to tie up scattered bits of accounting. It is the best introduction, not only to the many and important problems of cost accounting, but also to some phases of ordinary financial accounting. Examples are the accounts of departments and branches, i.e. of the subdivisions, for which separate data are recorded, that go to make up a large business. For here we are brought up against the problem of allocation. How should you split a common cost between departments? Ought you indeed to do it at all?

I would suggest that a plausible line of approach to the problem of allocation would be to try treating the departments of a business as if they were separate and competing units, i.e. as if the four walls of the firm enclosed an internal market. Economics have given us a fairly clear picture of how firms behave in the real (or 'external') market. Might not the same rules be extended to cover the subdivisions of a business - whether they be departments or processes or machines? We should then see that, although the money outlay on what is bought by the firm may be fixed, the corresponding services are not necessarily so. For instance, the rent paid for the whole shop may be fixed by a ten-year contract; but the manager is still free to rearrange the space between his departments. The latter will doubtless make 'bids' to him - whether in the form of vague cajolery for more space, or of forth-right offers to raise sales by £x if given another hundred square yards. When services can in this way be allocated as a matter of hard physical fact, the objections to allocating their cost seem to me to grow less. Instead, the process of allocating may serve to make the internal market more real, and to raise profits by ensuring that the firm's resources are split up between departments according to the best possible scheme of priorities. Of course, we might then find that our costs had been transformed. For a department's 'bids' for space and so on will presumably be less influenced by the actual costs - e.g. the rent paid to the landlord - than by what that space is nowadays worth, both in the outside and inside markets. The normal earning power of rival departments may well loom larger than the cost figures of the ledger. Once again we must choose between a backward- and a forward-looking approach. These two conflicting viewpoints seem indeed to lie at the very heart of nearly all our controversies.

The Contributions of Accounting to other Subjects

So far, I have tended to stress what the teacher of accounting can gain from his colleagues in nearby departments. Perhaps I may without too much immodesty drop some hint of the returns that accounting might make to its neighbours. What for instance might students of law and economics learn if their courses included accounting?

On the technical level, the returns seem so plain as to need no emphasis. Thus most lawyers will be helped if they can interpret company affairs or income tax rules in terms of figures. Again, statisticians are now experimenting with double-entry as a means for measuring national wealth, while economists seem to be adopting the balance sheet and other accounts as tools for their researchers.

But I believe accounting to be capable of more positive contributions. Might it not, for instance, give the economics student a clearer picture of how the business man's mind works - in particular, by showing in which fields his decisions can normally be guided by figures and in which by nothing less misty than his feelings. If I have grasped the matter aright, the economist explains the business man's activity by relating it to a quest for the level of output at which profits are at their peak. This view seems just as incontrovertible as the notion that a man tends to marry the person who will, he thinks, bring him most happiness. What should be made clear is that the business man is often no more likely than the suitor to be guided by schedules of costs. It is always risky to generalise on such topics; whatever one says, some member of the audience is fairly sure to reply: 'Our firm has for years done the exact opposite of what you suggest.' However, I venture to submit that most firms have not yet found the formal measurement of marginal costs and revenues to be feasible. This is not to say that the economics text-book is wrong to use such figures; they make the issue plainer, just as a psychologist's weighting of emotions might help us to understand other kinds of choice. But, being beset by so many unknowns, the business man can hardly do more than feel his way towards the output level that is suggested by common-sense modifications of past experience; he may reject alternatives by mental processes that do not reach the level of conscious thought, far less figures on paper. If his plans for the coming year ever reach the accounting stage, it will probably be only as a broad budget, showing the costs and revenues of what he assumes to be the best output.

Now comes another important point. A firm seldom makes the single product with which the teacher of economics - very rightly - introduces his disciples to the problem. Accordingly, when the business man has decided, however roughly, on his best general level of output for the future, he still has to allocate his efforts between his various products and departments. Here his accountant - and still more his cost accountant - does make formal comparisons of revenues and sacrifices. The cost accountant's usual method is, however, not to list all the possible alternatives and to show the most profitable; the number of unknowns and the range of permutations are so vast that such a procedure is often out of the question. If I am not mistaken, the cost accountant ought to sum up his work thus: 'You have given me - in the form of a master-budget for the year or some vaguer estimate - a picture of the total revenue that the best output may win; with the help of that picture, I must first express our varied products in terms of some common standard (such as the man-hour) and then show what revenue each of these units of work is expected to contribute towards our costs and dividends; armed with this figure of normal revenue, I shall test each activity to see if it is worthwhile.' In short, the cost accountant will feel much more at home with the economist when the latter is talking about normal revenue than when he is making marginal calculations.

In this matter - as in many others - accountants are influenced largely by their views on what is practicable. A university course in accounting must often follow this formula: First, what is ideal? Second, what data are at our disposal? Third, how far can we get towards the ideal on our limited material? Accounting may thus give a training whose attitude differs somewhat from that of its sister subjects; the student may receive a certain sense of urgency, of the need for reaching decision with the help of knowledge that is necessarily imperfect. In many branches of learning, a state of suspended judgement may well be the hall-mark of high scholarship; an accountant's clients expect advice by the first post to-morrow.

From what I have said about revenue, values and costs, it will be clear that, when the student of accounting is dealing with those parts of his subject, there is little risk of his being spoon-fed with something that has already been settled and reduced to cut-and-dried finality. But, if he will not be given the thrill of introduction to a complete and polished doctrinal structure, at least he may have the fun of ruminating over the questions that we - his elders and betters - have so far failed to answer, and of knowing that he may be the lucky prospector who will first strike gold. Most of the answers depend for proof, after all, not on advanced technicalities but on what men in general feel to be reasonable and useful. A student's mind is as good a jury as any on such points. Take for instance the fundamental question of value. I have said that man esteems things because they will yield him future benefits. But is it always so? Professor Bonbright tells us:

'A squirrel which betrays a high valuation for the nuts that he stores in the ground cannot confidently be said to base his conduct to the discounted present value that he attaches to the opportunity of securing a series of nourishing meals there from during the winter. Instead, the squirrel is apparently motivated by some impulse of a non-anticipating nature to get that nut to avoid eating it now, and to bury it in the ground.

'Human beings are doubtless more anticipatory than squirrels in their valuation processes. But it is an open question whether even men and women do not base their bids and offers for commodities partly on a similar impulse of desire for or aversion from the commodity itself, rather than on a process of valuing the prospects of a flow of future benefits. Can we be *confident that the impulse of a woman shopper which leads her to pay a certain price for a pretty dress or a delightful bottle of perfume is governed by her calculation of a series of future receipts of warmth and decoration, and a series of future receipts of pleasant smells and favourable social responses?'*

Please note, too, that values, costs and so forth are homely matters that the student will go on meeting long after he has left the class-room, and even if he does not earn his living at accounting. One hopes that he will be brought afresh to these topics every time that he makes his income-tax return or invests some money or even reads his newspaper, and that, accordingly, the issues will remain alive in his mind.

Conclusion

How shall I sum up this survey of accounting? A wit has said that the three fundamental questions of philosophy are 'how' 'why' and 'so what'? We might do worse than consider the way in which accounting deals with these three questions.

'How?' should present no difficulties. If instruction in accounting were merely a matter of describing a technique, any conscientious teacher could create a sound course out of the material at hand. But I have already made clear, I hope, that descriptive teaching is of inferior value. Only when the student is led to ask *'why?'* does he receive satisfactory stimulus to thought; this, too, he may get from accounting, but only if the teacher has a deep understanding of the administrative and legal aims that have moulded our mystery. Most important, is the student imbued with that power of making cool and detached criticisms which is implied by *'so what?'*? This is probably our weak point. Yet, when I remember how much of an accounting student's time may be spent in analysing the meaning of familiar but woolly ideas, in deciding whether the answer to an imposing mathematical calculation has any real significance, and in wrangling over these matters in the light of theories that themselves invite controversy, I feel not unhopeful about our future; I cannot but think that, with such a wealth of disputatious problems, accounting should be able to put students on guard mentally - though the instructor may well feel humble as he considers how hard it will be to create the body of principles that will act as his students' loadstone.

In short, I have little doubt that the subject of accounting is capable of becoming a worthy member of the academic syllabus. Whether it can do so in the hands of this particular teacher is of course another matter.

Notes

1.   Inaugural address delivered at the London School of Economics and Political Science (University of London) on 2nd December 1947. Sir Harold M Barton, F.C.A., was in the chair.

ACCOUNTING STANDARDS : A MIXED BLESSING?

Geoffrey Whittington

Introduction

In 1953, Professor Baxter wrote an article which was critical of the somewhat modest recommendations on accounting which were initiated in 1942 by the Institute of Chartered Accountants in England and Wales (ICAEW). In 1981, he repeated his critique, applying it to accounting standards which, by then, were issued in the UK by the Accounting Standards Committee (ASC), which was founded in 1970 (originally as the ASSC). This body was superseded by the Accounting Standards Board (ASB) in 1990. The ASB has greater resources, greater authority and a more ambitious programme than the ASC, including, for example, a substantial Statement of Principles. It seems likely that Professor Baxter's critique would apply more strongly to the ASB, and the present author, as a former pupil of Professor Baxter and a current member of the ASB, felt that it might be both appropriate and instructive to revisit the Baxter critique.

The natural prejudice of a member of the ASB is, of course, to defend the standard-setting process, but on a previous occasion the present author has found it necessary to recant an initially hostile reaction to one of Professor Baxter's critical essays (on the state of academic research: Baxter 1988, Whittington 1988 and 1995). Thus, the critique of standard-setting will be approached with due caution. First, we shall consider the original Baxter critique (1953), followed by its later application to standard-setting (1981). Next, the author will attempt to defend the accounting standard-setting process, particularly in the context of the ASB. Finally, we shall consider what lessons the standard-setter can learn from the Baxter critique.

The original Baxter critique of recommendations on accounting theory (1953)

The title of Professor Baxter's 1953 critique is significant. It refers to "recommendations on accounting

theory (emphasises added), whereas the ICAEW pronouncements were "recommendations on accounting **principles**". The distinction is an important one because principles, as pronounced by the ICAEW, were essentially guides to action and did not necessarily have a strong theoretical base: generalisation of existing practice and the subjective judgments of members of the committee were at least as important an ingredient as theoretical reasoning in drafting the recommendations. This was acknowledged by Professor Baxter, but it was the theoretical element of which he was particularly critical:

> "A recommendation tends to contain three types of ingredient:
>
> (1)   A description of the given problem;
>
> (2)   A reasoned discussion, often based on fundamentals, on how best to solve the problem; and
>
> (3)   The recommended solution.
>
> It is mainly (2) that seems objectionable. For here the accounting society weighs intellectual principles, analyses the *pros* and *cons* of the alternative arguments, and decides that one view is better than the others; in short, here authority tells us what is true. Is it wise for any group of men to say what is "true" or "right" in matters of theory?"

(Baxter, 1953, p.415)

He goes on to say "By "theory" I mean the attempt to explain, in terms of fundamentals, what accounting is and what it tries to do". He contrasts theory-based recommendations with "working rules" which he associates only with ingredient (3), solutions "designed to make something run smoothly", and which he regards as acceptable. He recognises that theory influences the choice of rules, but believes that their acceptance "should not imply that the official seal of approval has been put on any theory". In the context of published accounting statements, he believes that rules "should not only avoid **why**, but should be chary about **how**. The stress should be on **what**". Thus, minimum disclosure rules are to be welcomed, but the prescription of methods, particularly relating to valuation, is to be avoided:

"A terse list of minimum requirements, such as is given in the British Companies Act,
works well and leaves honest men tolerably free to think and experiment. It provides
a floor, not a ceiling."

(Baxter, 1953, p.416)

After acknowledging the benefits of the ICAEW recommendations as "private forerunners and
reinforcements to the law", Baxter mounts his case against recommendations insofar as they relate to
theory:

"The case against official recommendations on theory is threefold. First, men do not always
become better at research when they work as a group. Second, if authority takes direct part
in the pursuit of truth, it may hinder rather than help. Third - and most important - there are no
sure signs by which truth can be recognised."

(Baxter, 1953, p.420)

The essence of this argument is that statements on theoretical matters by professional committees may
stifle new ideas:

"Privilege is bad for ideas as for men; only if they can jostle one another in a democratic way
is the best likely to reach the top"   (Baxter, 1953, p.422)

Since knowledge in all fields of study develops through time, authoritative statements may freeze the
profession's state of knowledge in some form of current conventional wisdom which will rapidly become
out-dated. Baxter quotes Bacon's memorable aphorism "Truth is the daughter, not of Authority, but of
Time". It is argued that this effect of recommendations damages education, giving rise to "minds less
fit to solve the new problems of tomorrow", constrains the ability of the practising accountant to innovate
(as in the case of the SEC preventing price change accounting adjustments in the USA in 1947), and
restricts the independence of judgment of the auditor.

Baxter goes on to discuss recommendations relating to definitions and standard practice. He acknowledges that clarity of definition can ease the exchange of ideas, but fears that even here official pronouncements can stifle evolution, since definitions are rarely free of theoretical judgements. In the case of standard practice, he is happier that recommendations should influence the form and content of financial statements than that they should restrict or determine the methods of measurement used. He also believes that standards should be guides to usual practice rather than a guide to what is necessarily right. The paper ends with a statement of Baxter's general concern that official pronouncements on matters of accounting theory will stifle the education and professional development of accountants.

> ".... a group of men who resign their hard problems to others must eventually give up all claim to be a learned profession."

(Baxter, 1953, p.427)

The subsequent introduction of the accounting standards programme in 1970 increased the number, the authority, and the theoretical content of accounting standards. We now turn to Professor Baxter's critique of this system.

The Baxter critique of Accounting Standards (1981)

Professor Baxter's paper "Accounting Standards - Boon or Curse?" was based on a lecture given in New York. It therefore refers to the USA system of standard-setting (as did the previous Baxter critique) as well as to that of the UK, but, for the purposes of the present paper, we shall concentrate on its application to the UK.

The paper opens with a review of recent (as of 1981) standard-setting developments. The ASC had issued an important body of standards and had achieved substantial compliance with them, assisted by the support of the professional bodies and the Stock Exchange. The ASC's greatest difficulty had been encountered in dealing with price change accounting. The current cost accounting standard (SSAP16, 1980) had just been promulgated, and there were threats of non-compliance, but generally the ASC seemed to be effective. It was only later, in the mid 1980's, that SSAP16 collapsed, due to serious non-compliance, and creative accounting emerged as a serious problem.[2]

Professor Baxter's critique of accounting standards starts with the three-fold distinction which he made previously in the context of accounting recommendations, and a repetition of his exhortation that accounting standard-setters (or drafters of recommendations) should concentrate on the third aspect, the solution ("rules of action"), and avoid pronouncements on theoretical issues. He then turns to a new analysis of standards, based on the classification of standards by his colleague Harold Edey (1977). This four-fold classification of standards can be summarised as follows:

Type 1 : Disclosure of accounting policies

Type 2 : Uniformity of layout and presentation

Type 3 : Disclosure of specific matters

Type 4 : Measurement methods

It is the **Type 4** standard about which Baxter expresses serious doubts, because the choice of measurement method inevitably involves a choice between competing theories. A conceptual framework is described as "a fearsome extension of **Type 4**" (Baxter, 1981, p.6).

There follows a brief respite for the standard-setter, in the form of a short section on "the good side of standards". "They give us handy rules for our daily work", especially if they are of types 1 to 3. They also foster comparability, but the praise for this is faint: "there is even something to be said for the view that it is better if all firms issue second-rate figures on the same basis than first-rate figures on conflicting bases" (p.7). Standards also "force our weaker brethren to improve their work". However, the author is unimpressed by the claim that **type 4** standards can improve measures of value.

"The grounds for doubt" are then expressed under seven headings, which can be summarised as follows:

(1) Standards are costly.

(2) Standards may become petrified and so impede progress.

(3) Accounting figures do not lend themselves to standardisation, because of differences between different firms, industries and users.

(4) Standards pose difficulties of interpretation which may give opportunities for what is sometimes called loop-holing, ie exploiting ambiguities to avoid the intended consequences of the standard.

(5) Standard-making may become politicised.

(6) "The essence of a profession is surely that each member is willing to think and judge for himself about matters of principle".

(7) Even if standards lay down principles, they will still leave scope for subjective judgment on matters of measurement.

The conclusion is that "standards will bring many setbacks and much disillusion" (p.8). Professor Baxter then reiterates some of the views of his 1953 paper, on the provisional nature of any theoretical view and the need for ideas to compete freely. He compares accounting standards with the rules of medieval gilds. He states that "a theorist must suspect that by the tests of both logic and history, **type 4** standards are inherently defective; other men are more likely to view the defects not as fundamental but as remedial faults of draughting or detail" (p.9). He then turns to four suggested ways in which the dangers in accounting standards could be lessened:

(1) Authoritative pronouncements on principle should be avoided.

(2) **Type 4** standards (on measurement) should be avoided.

(3) "A standard should not pander to political ends"

and (4) "standards should be explained in terms of **normal behaviour**" rather than principles.

The paper concludes with a gloomy view of the effects of accounting standards on the education of accountants". "Now that we are substituting rules of thumb for reason, one must sadly conclude that the critics" (of accounting as an academic discipline) "were right" (p.10).

A defence of accounting standards

An accounting academic who is also involved in accounting standard-setting will inevitably find this message unpalatable, especially if the standard-setting body to which he belongs is constructing a conceptual framework (the ASB's statements of principles) which Professor Baxter described as "a fearsome extension of **Type 4**", his least favoured form of standard. Professor Baxter is, however, a wily opponent, who knows his ground extremely well, so that his would-be critic needs to spy out the land rather carefully before rushing into the attack. The most obvious feature of his position is that, like a good general, he has already conceded the ground that is least defensible: he is willing, for the most part, to accept standards relating to format and disclosure. Measurement standards are much less acceptable, and strong objection is made to supporting particular theories rather than simply promulgating rules.

In conceding this ground, Professor Baxter has effectively accepted the case for **some** form of accounting standard-setting. The matter at issue is precisely what form this should take. In particular, should accounting standards be justified or explained by theoretical argument and should their scope extend to matters of measurement? However, before addressing these issues, it is important to understand the case for accounting standards which is accepted in the Baxter papers. This hinges on two benefits . First, accounting standards aid communication and comparability by creating a common language. Second, standards "force our weaker brethren to improve their work" (Baxter, 1981, p.7), by requiring a minimum quantity and quality of accounting information.

The first of these benefits, the improvement of the effectiveness of accounts as a means of communication, has been argued eloquently by William Baxter's former colleague, the late David

28

Solomons, who did much to advance the cause of standard-setting both in the UK and in the USA. Solomons (1989, p.6)[3] regards accounting standards as a natural extension of the statutory regulation contained in the Companies Act, an argument accepted by Baxter (1953, p.416) insofar as **"Type 1"** to **"Type 3"** standards are concerned. He also invokes "the virtues of comparability, standardization and credibility". He lays great stress on comparability: "good accounting standards make **like** things look alike". This argument was accepted by Baxter, albeit somewhat grudgingly, in his statement (1981, p.7) that it might be better for all firms to issue second-rate figures on the same basis than first-rate figures on a conflicting basis. Solomons' second virtue, standardization, refers to economies of processing by the user, as in an alphabetical listing rather than a random listing of entries in a telephone directory. This would seem to fall into Baxter's category of "handy rules for our daily work".

The second benefit of accounting standards, providing minimum standards for the "weaker brethren", relates to Solomons' third virtue, credibility. In practice, this has been probably the most significant factor in the drive for accounting standards in the UK and in the many other countries which have adopted them, typically on a private sector self-regulatory basis. Critics of accounting standards, such as Arthur Morison (1970) (cited with approval in Baxter, 1981) and William Baxter tend to give insufficient emphasis to the credibility problem, and, in particular, to the damage to the credibility of accounting and auditing which can be caused by the behaviour of a few "weaker brethren" who attempt to free-ride on the good reputation painstakingly built up by others. Accounting standard-setting systems have often been created to deal with perceived abuses, and "scandals" have often been the critical events which have triggered important events in standard-setting such as the foundation of the ASSC by the chartered accountancy bodies in 1970.[4]

The credibility issue not only explains a substantial part of the motivation for the voluntary adoption of accounting standards by the profession, but it also brings into question the assumptions made by William Baxter, Arthur Morison and others, who criticise accounting standards for their potentially inhibiting role on the independent exercise of professional judgment. This view is argued eloquently by Morison:

"The power of free and rational argument remains, I am old-fashioned enough to believe, the best road to the truth in human affairs. I would therefore give companies the maximum freedom to present their accounts in whatever way they thought fit, and would then require them to **explain** and **justify** the course they had taken. The auditor's task - no light one! - would be to ensure that they did. And to see that they did it fairly."

(Morison, 1970, p.281)

It may be no coincidence that William Baxter and Arthur Morison were both trained as Scottish chartered accountants. The tradition of the Scottish profession has always been to lay great stress upon the importance of independent professional judgment, and the importance of education in equipping professionals for that responsibility. Hence, Scotland has a strong tradition of practitioner/academics, recent examples being David Flint and Sir John Shaw, who have each had careers as senior practitioners, presidents of their Institute and university professors: an unheard of combination in England. Unfortunately, however, the English way has tended to prevail in recent years and has, in many respects, followed the American way. Accounting and auditing are now big business, and practitioners crave standards, either to guide and justify their own judgments or to keep the standards of their competitors up to the mark. This change of climate is described by another distinguished Scottish Accountant, Sir William Slimmings (1981) in his account of the Scottish contribution to the foundation of the ASSC.

"His" (Arthur Morison's) "condition for allowing the maximum flexibility in the preparation of accounts was that those responsible for the accounts should explain and justify what they had done. This just had not happened in practice. If it had, it would inevitably have thrown up the 'great many permissable accounting conventions' to which he referred, and would have focused much earlier attention on the question as to whether the 'great many' were not too many".

(Slimmings, 1981, p.16)

An anecdotal, but vivid, demonstration of the change of climate is that one of the most distinguished of the current generation of Scottish chartered accountants, Sir David Tweedie, a former pupil of David Flint and technical partner of Arthur Morison's firm[5], is now Chairman of the Accounting Standards Board, which is developing both statements of principles and standards on measurement. Thus accounting standards have to be designed to meet the needs of the imperfect world in which they are applied, rather than an ideal world in which they would not be necessary.

Thus, one reason for questioning Professor Baxter's critique of accounting standards may be that it applies in conditions which, however desirable in theory, do not exist in practice. However, it is also possible to question the Baxter critique from a more fundamental standpoint: that it is not possible strictly to separate disclosure and format from measurement or rules from theory. That Professor Baxter himself recognises this potential weakness is apparent in his comments on standards of **Types 2** and **3**, where he recognises the possibility of underpinnings in theory and difficulties of separation from **Type 4** (measurement issues).

The essence of the problem is that rules are underpinned by theory, and that this applies to matters of format and disclosure as well as to matters of measurement. For example, if we consider the recent work of the ASB, its most striking contribution on matters of format has probably been FRS3, Reporting Financial Performance (1992). This provides a new format for the profit and loss account, including a statement of total recognised gains and losses, which yields what is sometimes called a comprehensive income measure. FRS3 also requires new disclosures in the form of dis-aggregation of some important aspects of an entity's performance, notably the separation of continuing operations and the contribution of new acquisitions. The stated objective is "to aid users in understanding the performance achieved by a reporting entity in a period and to assist them in forming a basis for their assessment of future results and cash flows". Clearly, this indicates a theoretical view of the role of accounts: the object is not merely to record past transactions but also to do it in a manner which is intended to aid an understanding of performance and provide a basis for assessing future performance. Such a theoretical position, if held consistently, is likely to have implications not only for format and disclosure but also for measurement. Thus, developing a coherent standard on format, involves the theoretical underpinnings which Professor Baxter would prefer to avoid.

FRS5, Reporting the Substance of Transactions illustrates this point even more vividly. This standard is designed to deal with various complex transactions, such as off-balance sheet financing, which had come to be regarded as creative accounting devices. In the case of off-balance sheet financing, FRS5 can be regarded principally as a disclosure standard. It restores the relevant assets and liabilities to the balance sheet by invoking what lawyers would describe as the principle of substance over form. In order to implement this principle, it is necessary to refer to the definitions of assets and liabilities contained in the ASB's Statement of Principles. Assets, for example, are defined as "Rights or other access to future economic benefits controlled by an entity as a result of past transactions or events". This definition provides a theoretical underpinning which must affect many aspects of accounting, including measurement.

Although FRS5 appears superficially to be a long standard it is, in concept, very simple and the simplicity derives from its conceptual basis. Its length derives from the application notes which illustrate the application of the concepts to particular situations. In the absence of the concepts a much longer rule book would be required to deal with all conceivable situations rather than merely with the chosen illustrations. Moreover, in the absence of an underlying conceptual basis, the rules would appear to be arbitrary, potentially inconsistent with one another, and incapable of adaptation to meet the needs of new situations arising from the novel financial instruments and other arrangements which are constantly being created by innovative financial markets. In such an environment, it is difficult to see how Professor Baxter's ideal form of standards, ie rules without theory, would be workable. Moreover, his injunction to justify standards in terms of generally accepted practice is impossible to apply where there is no generally accepted practice, because the problem arises from financial innovation.

This leads to the more general case for adopting that "fearsome extension of **Type 4**", the conceptual framework. Professor Baxter himself quotes the description of a camel as "a horse designed by a committee". Accounting standards, whether designed by a committee or by different individuals acting in an uncoordinated manner, are likely to lack coherence if they are not based on common view of the purpose of accounts, the nature of the business entity, and other fundamental issues. The lack of coherence matters for two reasons. First, if we take the negative view of standards, that they are there to keep the "weaker brethren" in line, inconsistency between standards facilitates "loop-holing", ie structuring financial arrangements in such a way that they fall within standards that give favourable treatment.[6] Second, if we take the positive view of standards, that they are there to facilitate the provision of useful information, it seems likely that this will be aided by standards which have a common set of underlying principles, rather than selecting the treatment of different types of transaction on the basis of entirely different assumptions and objectives. Thus, a statement of principles, or conceptual framework , can aid the effectiveness of accounting standards.

What we can learn from the Baxter critique

Having offered a defence of accounting standards, and particularly of the **Type 4** variety and its "fearsome extension", it is now necessary to consider what we can learn from Professor Baxter's critique. He is a thoughtful critic, not by instinct opposed to accounting theory, and well disposed to the improvement of accounting practice. We must therefore take his criticisms very seriously and attempt to meet them.

At the centre of Professor Baxter's critique is an anxiety that a conceptual framework will inhibit the development of accounting though and that accounting standards will have a similar effect on innovation in accounting practice. He perceives that these adverse effects will be worse, the greater the authority of the standard-setting body. Given the rudimentary development of accounting theory (the subject having developed as a university discipline mainly during Professor Baxter's lifetime, and in no small part in the UK, due to his personal efforts), his anxiety about inhibiting further development is well founded. Equally, his anxiety about inhibiting developments in practice is well founded, given the competitive pressures on auditors and the current fear of litigation, which encourage the auditor to hide behind the rule book. What, then, should be done to alleviate these anxieties if we accept that, in an imperfect world, some form of accounting standards is necessary and the standards are more likely to be effective if they are based on a common set of principles?

The four ameliorative measures suggested in Baxter (1981, p.10) have already been cited.

The first, the avoidance of authoritative statements on principle, seems a conceptual framework. However, the word **authoritative** is important. It may help matters if statements of principles, such as those issued by the ASB, are regarded not as being definitive pronouncements on theory but rather as **provisional** principles adopted to add coherence to work on the current standards programme, but not intended to inhibit debate or future development. Fortunately, this is the current status of the ASB's statement of principles. Nevertheless, it must be conceded that there is a serious danger that such statements will, nevertheless, become an orthodoxy which inhibits future progress. It is therefore incumbent on bodies such as the ASB to revisit and revise their statements of principles on a regular basis.

The second, the avoidance of standards on measurement, seems difficult to implement. As already explained, measurement is bound up intimately with other aspects of accounting standards. However, as the experience of price change accounting has demonstrated, measurement is certainly one of the more difficult and controversial issues facing the standard-setter. Thus, Professor Baxter's critique warns us to approach measurement issues with particular caution and, where possible, allow scope for practice to evolve. This approach has been adopted hitherto by the ASB, which has preferred evolution to revolution in the introduction of current values.

The third measure, not pandering to political ends is, on one level highly desirable and, on another impossible. Clearly, a standard-setting body should not allow itself to be captured by a particular interest group, if it is supposed to be serving the wider community. The constitution of the ASB guards against this possibility by the broad membership of the governing body, the Financial Reporting Council (FRC), which has representatives of all of the main groups affected by accounting standards (including government, industry, the accounting profession, investors and trade unions). However, it is inevitable that standard-setters will have to make judgments which affect different interest groups in different ways, ie they will face problems of social choice. Thus, we cannot avoid the political nature of standard-setting, although we might hope that it is exercised in a manner which is seen by the groups concerned to be reasonably even-handed in accordance with the constitution of the standard-setting body. William Baxter's former colleague, David Solomons, was a keen advocate of accounting standards and was also a strong believer that standards should be apolitical. He drew an analogy with map-making: maps should be accurate representations of physical reality and accounts should be accurate representations of economic reality (Solomons, 1983). Unfortunately, even maps can be affected by political judgments, notably when they delineate the boundaries of countries, and the economic claims expressed in accounts are at least as contentious and difficult to measure as the territorial claims expressed in political maps. Thus, although standard-setters may aspire to objectivity where it is possible, they cannot escape the "political" issues of social choice, about which they will be lobbied constantly by their constituency, eg on such issues as the burden on small businesses or the international competitive position of certain industries, which will be affected by the application of certain accounting standards.

The fourth measure, explaining standards in terms of normal behaviour rather than principles, appears to be inconsistent with using a statement of principles as a guide, as does the ASB. Not only would the criterion of "normal behaviour" lead to piecemeal and potentially inconsistent standards, but it would afford no guide to improving standards where "normal behaviour" was felt to be inadequate or where guidance was required on a novel type of transaction for which there was no established practice. Moreover, there is a considerable variety of behaviour observable in practice, and the selection of what is normal is a matter of judgment which might itself be best guided by some principles.

However, it may be that "normal behaviour" can enter into the standard-setting process by a more subtle route, by guiding the selection of principles. If principles have a theoretical basis, which is what Professor Baxter fears, there are two broad ways in which they can derived: deductive theories derived from assumptions and inductive theories derived from generalisations of empirical observation of practice. It is the former type which Professor Baxter would seem to fear most, because it is heavily laden with subjective assumptions. On the other hand, it is the latter, principles derived inductively from observation, which tend to underlie the debates of standard-setters and professional bodies (Whittington, 1986). Such principles as matching, accruals and prudence are derived from generalisations of practice: a classic example of this type of work is Paton and Littleton (1940), which has had a clear influence on subsequent conceptual frameworks, such as those of the FASB, the IASC and the ASB.

A measure which is not on Professor Baxter's list but is mentioned in his work is that accounting standards should set **minimum** levels ("a floor, not a ceiling") and should not prevent **additional** disclosure. A related concept, which is embodied in UK law and practice, is the **true and fair over-ride**, ie accounts can depart from standard practice if this is considered necessary to present a true and fair view of the affairs of the business. These two safeguards together should prevent companies or auditors from being inhibited from expressing themselves as they would wish in their reports and accounts. Of course, they will not **encourage** freedom of expression or imaginative innovations in financial reporting, but at lease they will serve to avoid the worst of the damage which standardisation might cause.

Conclusion

Professor Baxter's original eloquent critique of accounting standards (1953), although written when the state of auditing, accounting and accounting standards was very different, was perceptive enough to disturb the complacency of the accounting standard-setter more than forty years later. His fundamental attachment to the liberal values of free discussion supported by a sound education must be shared by any academic who is seriously concerned to follow in his footsteps in developing accounting as an academic discipline and as a learned profession. In the same spirit of free discussion, the present paper has attempted to evaluate the relevance of the Baxter critique to the present-day situation, particularly in the context of the work of the ASB.

It has been argued that accounting standards are necessary and that an underlying conceptual framework is desirable, but that we must attempt to avoid the consequent dangers identified by the Baxter critique and attempt to deal with them. Important avoidance measures which may help include emphasising the provisional nature of statements of principles, deriving such principles, where possible, by the inductive generalisation of current practice rather than deductive reasoning from normative assumptions, encouraging disclosure of forms or types of information beyond the minimum required by standards, and, perhaps most of all, retaining the "true and fair" over-ride, which allows standard requirements to be over-ruled when accountants and auditors are willing to justify their judgment as being better, in a particular situation, than that of the standard-setter.

References

Accounting Standards Board (1992), FRS3, Reporting Financial Performance (ASB, London).

Accounting Standards Board (1994), FRS5, Reporting the Substance of Transactions (ASB, London).

Accounting Standards Board (1995), Exposure Draft, Statement of Principles for Financial Reporting (ASB, London).

Accounting Standards Committee (1980), SSAP16, Current Cost Accounting (ASC, London).

Baxter, W.T. (1953), 'Recommendations on Accounting Theory', reprinted in Baxter and Davidson (1962), pp. 414-427.

Baxter, W.T. (1981), 'Accounting Standards - Boon or Curse?', Accounting and Business Research (Winter), pp. 3-10.

Baxter, W.T. (1988), Accounting Research - Academic Tends versus Practical Needs, The Institute of Chartered Accountants of Scotland, Edinburgh.

Baxter, W.T. and S. Davidson (eds) (1962), Studies in Accounting Theory (Sweet & Maxwell, London).

Baxter, W.T. and S. Davidson (eds) (1977), Studies in Accounting (The Institute of Chartered Accountants in England and Wales, London).

Edey, H.C. (1977), 'Accounting Standards in the British Isles', in Baxter and Davidson (1977), pp. 294-305.

Hanson, J.D. (1989), 'Developments in Financial Reporting Practice over the last 20 years', in Tonkin and Skerratt (1989), pp. 1-66.

Leach, R. and E. Stamp (eds) (1981), British Accounting Standards, the first 10 years (Woodland-Faulkner, Cambridge).

Morison, A.M.C. (1970), The Role of the Reporting Accountant Today', reprinted in Baxter and Davidson (1977), pp. 265-293.

Paton, W.A. and A.C. Littleton (1940), An Introduction to Corporate Accounting Standards, (American Accounting Association, Sarasota).

Slimmings, W. (1981), 'The Scottish Contribution', in Leach and Stamp (1981), pp. 12-26.

Solomons, D. (1983), 'the Political Implications of Accounting and Accounting Standard Setting', Accounting and Business Research (Spring), pp. 107-118.

Solomons, D. (1986), Making Accounting Policy: The Quest for Credibility in Financial Reporting (Oxford University Press, New York).

Solomons, D. (1989), Guidelines for Financial Reporting Standards (The Institute of Chartered Accountants in England and Wales, London).

Stamp, E. and C. Marley (1970), Accounting Principles and the City Code: The Case for Reform (Butterworth, London).

Tonkin, J.D. and L.C.L. Skerratt (eds) (1989), Financial Reporting 1988-89: A Survey of UK Accounting Practice (The Institute of Chartered Accountants in England and Wales, London).

Tweedie, D.P. and G. Whittington (1990), 'Financial Reporting: Current Problems and their Implications for Systematic Reform', <u>Accounting and Business Research</u> (Winter), pp. 87-102.

Whittington, G. (1986), 'Financial Accounting Theory: An Overview', <u>The British Accounting Review</u> (Autumn), pp. 4-41.

Whittington, G. (1988), Review of Baxter (1988), <u>Accounting and Business Research</u> (Summer), p. 267.

Whittington, G. (1995), <u>Is Accounting Becoming too Interesting?</u> The Sir Julian Hodge Lecture (University College of Wales, Aberystwyth).

Notes

1. A helpful review of the ASC's achievement is provided by Hanson (1989).

2. Solomons' views were developed much more fully in his 1986 book, Making Accounting Policy: The Quest for Credibility in Financial Reporting.

3. See, for example, the campaigning book by Stamp and Marley (1970). The ASSC was the predecessor of the ASC.

4. Thomson McLintock & Co. A further sign of the change of climate is that this firm has now been absorbed into KPMG, a giant international auditing firm which has recently formed a company to undertake its larger audits and thus gain the benefit of limited liability.

5. Tweedie and Whittington (1990) explore the deficiencies of financial reporting at the time when the ASB was established and attempt to identify the conceptual issues underlying these deficiencies.

THE CONCEPTUAL FRAMEWORK AND THE ACCOUNTING STANDARDS BOARD

Sir David Tweedie

1. The Problems of the Accounting Standards Committee

The Accounting Standards Board (ASB) was conceived by the Dearing Committee in the late 1980s. The previous few years had not been glorious ones for the British accounting profession and, in particular, for the standard-setting process. The problems were not caused by the individual standard-setters but by the system within which they had to operate. Indeed, in its final years, the Accounting Standards Committee (ASC) had a fine reputation and was extremely prolific, but simply did not have the ability to protect its standards from outside interference or to ensure that its standards were obeyed. Consequently, the process itself was discredited. The problems were essentially four-fold.

i. Dissipated authority

Until 1990 accounting standards (Statements of Standard Accounting Practice (SSAPs)) were not issued by the standard-setting body but by the individual accounting institutes. These institutes had the final say on a standard and if an institute's authorising body (normally its Council) disagreed with an SSAP then invariably some changes would have to be made to accommodate the institute's views (even if these changes were to be against the wishes of ASC itself). Lowest common denominator standards were inevitable!

ii. The problem of the precedent

The true and fair view has been described by Hoffman and Arden (1983) as being ambulatory. The content of true and fair is constantly moving. What was true and fair at the time of the 1948 Companies Act would certainly not be considered so by the financial community today - measurement techniques and the volume of disclosure have been transformed in the last 50 years. However, while 'true and fair' is a moving concept, it can sometimes wander from what some may deem to be the path of righteousness and enter dangerous territory. Truth and fairness comprises not only accounting requirements of law and accounting standards but also accepted practice. Consequently, a dubious practice, which was not against the requirements of any standard or the law, even though it may have been against the spirit of both, could become accepted. Provided that several major companies had prepared accounts adopting the practice and major firms of auditors had accepted it, it was very difficult for later preparers and auditors to repudiate the practice, and in particular for an auditor to qualify on the grounds that the accounts incorporating the scheme did not show a true and fair view.

The mid-80's was a prime period for creative accounting. In the City of London ingenious schemes were devised to increase profit or to improve balance sheet gearing, for example, by deeming convertible debt to be equity or by removing liabilities off-balance sheet in order to flatter the financial statements[7]. A robust stand by the accounting profession at an early stage might well have prevented these schemes developing into precedents which many Finance directors and auditors reluctantly had to accept. The auditors of ten years ago, however, were not as confident as their counterparts of today and practices were accepted which in 1996 would be repudiated by finance directors and, in any event, stamped upon by auditors. Sadly in the 1980s, these precedents, once established, became the basis for other, often even more disreputable, schemes - the profession's "Creeping Crumple" had begun!

iii. No enforcement mechanism

The ASC could not insist on its standards being observed. While the accounting institutes expected their members to observe SSAPs, in practice, the standards would only be obeyed if they commanded general acceptance. It was thought that if an SSAP were to be challenged by the united ranks of the big auditing firms and the major listed companies, the SSAP would have difficulty obtaining acceptance and if companies refused to adopt it and auditors refused to qualify their opinion on the financial statements, then the Standard would fall into disrepute. This essentially is what happened with the gradual demise of SSAP 16, 'Current cost accounting'. SSAP 16 appeared in 1980 when inflation was already receding and gradually companies stopped complying with the standard with the result that it had to be withdrawn.

The withdrawal of SSAP 16 ended an unhappy era for the Accounting Standards Committee's attempts to deal with price-level accounting commencing with the Government's repudiation in 1973-74 of PSSAP 7 (the 'P' stood for provisional) which the accountancy profession was warned not to issue as a full Standard given the Government's intention to set up a Committee of Enquiry into inflation accounting - the Sandilands Committee which eventually rejected current purchasing power accounting (the thrust of PSSAP 7) and advocated current cost accounting. The rejection in 1977 by members of the English Institute at a Special Meeting[8] of the Exposure Draft (ED 18) prepared by the Accounting Standards Committee based on the findings of the Sandilands Committee was the beginning of the standard-setters' loss of power[9].

iv. Inconsistent standards

The Accounting Standards Committee's budget in 1989 was only some £440,000 per annum (compared with the 1995 budget of £1.8m per annum for the Accounting Standards Board). It had very scarce resources and, to augment these, standards were usually prepared by working parties of unpaid volunteers. These working parties, usually consisting of different individuals on each occasion, not unnaturally had dissimilar ideas about accounting. Consequently, standards were sometimes drawn up on inconsistent principles. For example, while SSAP 24 'Accounting for pension costs' required a charge for pension costs to be put through the profit and loss account, SSAP 15 'Accounting for deferred tax', frequently, would not allow any resulting tax relief to be recorded.

2. The Dearing Committee

The Dearing Committee (1988) looked at all the above issues and came forward with recommendations, almost all of which were accepted both by the profession and Government, the latter enacting the principal proposals enabling the ASB to begin work on 1st August 1990. The Committee dealt with the principal proposals enabling the ASB to begin work on 1st August 1990. The Committee dealt with the first three problems by proposing that:

the ASB should have the right to set its own standards, thereby removing the veto power of the six accountancy institutes;

an Urgent Issues Task Force should be created with the ability to issue pronouncements at short notice to stamp out the flow of precedents which had disfigured accounting in the mid-1980s; and

a Financial Reporting Review Panel should be instituted to enforce Board's standards, the legal status of which, as stated by Mary Arden in Opinion (see the Foreword to Accounting Standards, 1993, pp 17-18), had been enhanced by the changes in the standard-setting process which no longer represented only the views of the accounting profession but also those of the representatives of the business and financial community.

"Experience and legislative history ... have both illustrated the subtlety and evolving nature of the relationship between law and accounting practice. Accounting standards are now assured as an authoritative source of the latter. In consequence it is now the norm for accounts to comply with accounting standards. I would add this. Just as a custom which is upheld by the courts may properly be regarded as a source of law, so too, in my view does an accounting standard which the court holds must be complied with to meet the true and fair requirement become, in cases where it is applicable, a source of law in itself in the widest sense of that term". Arden (1993), para 15.

The backing for the Board's work had been immeasurably strengthened by the changes brought about by the Dearing Report. The recommendation of the Dearing Committee however that is of most interest to us in this Paper is its proposals to remove the fourth problem facing the ASC - inconsistent standards. The Committee suggested that the Accounting Standards Board should commence work on a conceptual framework - a means of providing a consistent basis for accounting standards:

"7.2   Our conclusion is that the lack of a conceptual framework is a handicap to those involved in setting accounting standards as well as to those applying them. Work on its development should, therefore, be pursued at a higher rate than hitherto but consistent with the perceived scope for progress. We do not see advantage in a large scale expenditure programme at this stage of the development of thinking. But we do recommend that work should be undertaken on a modest scale, building on the work already done in the United States, by the IASC and elsewhere, with scope for an enlarged allocation resource when the Proposed Financial Reporting Council ... judges there to be a reasonable basis for substantial progress. We believe that work in this area will assist standard setters in formulating their thinking on particular accounting issues, facilitate judgements on the sufficiency of the disclosures required to give a true and fair view, and assist preparers and auditors in interpreting accounting standards and in resolving accounting issues not dealt with by specific standards.

7.3   Whether or not a conceptual framework is successfully developed, we recommend that when accounting standards are issued they should be accompanied by a statement of the principles underlying them and of the reasons why alternatives were rejected, so that those with a duty to apply standards can do so with better understanding and accordingly improve the quality of their decisions" Dearing (1988).

3.   The beginnings of the Statement of Principles

The ASB resolved at its first meetings in 1990 to commence work on a Conceptual Framework. It was determined that this Framework would be used to introduce consistency into accounting standards setting. It was thought, however, that the title "a conceptual framework", would be deemed to be off-puffing by many accountants who had not been trained in accounting theory. The term, "Statement of Principles", was therefore derived from para 7.3 of the Dearing Report as few accountants would argue against financial reporting being based on consistent principles.

The Board was, however, concerned with the potential resource commitment involved in such a project. The impressive work undertaken by the Financial Accounting Standards Board in the USA had been both time consuming and expensive - a past Research Director of the FASB has been quoted as saying that about one third of the FASB's resources were devoted to the conceptual projects. Given that the annual resources of the FASB in the early 1990s amounted to £14 million per annum compared with the ASB's £1.5m or so, the Board was not equipped to undertake an exercise similar to that of the Americans. Indeed, as shown above, this had not been the intention of the Dearing Committee.

The Board however had the advantage of the existence, not only of the FASB Conceptual Framework (Statements of Financial Accounting Concepts 1-6, 1978-1985), but also the newly completed IASC Framework (1989), and the brief Financial Statement Concepts produced by the Canadians (1991) [Handbook Section 1000]. In addition, the Australian standard-setter was working on its own Conceptual Framework and at the time of the Board's institution in 1990, had already issued three final Statements of Accounting Concepts [SACs 1-3] namely SAC 1 'Definition of the Reporting Entity'; SAC 2 'Objective of General Purpose Financial Reporting'; and SAC 3 'Qualitative Characteristics of Financial Information' while work was under way on the critical statement concerned with the elements of financial statements [eventually SAC 4 'Definition and Recognition of the Elements of Financial Statements' published in 1992]. See Tweedie, (1991) pp.13-15.

The Board, however, faced a dilemma. On the one hand the danger of not immediately commencing work on a conceptual statement was clear - accounting standards might be issued, which later, if found to be inconsistent with the Statement of Principles, would have to be revised relatively soon after issue to the Board's discredit and to the cost of industry. On the other hand, given that the Board had been set up because of the creative accounting of the 1980s and the demand for change, to spend its first few years working hard on the Statement of Principles to the exclusion of all else would have led it to fail in one of its prime objectives. While, after some three years of its existence, the Board did eventually face complaints about "overloading" preparers with its pronouncements, I suspect these criticisms would have paled into insignificance if no standard had been produced for four or five years![10]

The Board, therefore, decided on a twin track approach. It debated the major substantive issues of British financial reporting and determined its overall work programme. In conjunction with this programme, the Statement of Principles was to be developed in parallel with those standards which would be affected by its main conclusions. (Appendix I)

A guide to the work necessary had been given by an examination of the then extant conceptual frameworks. Not surprisingly, given the pioneering work of the FASB, there was a commonality in the main features of these frameworks. Seven main areas had been considered by the various standard-setters, namely:

1.   The objective of financial reporting,

2.   Qualitative characteristics of accounting information;

3.   The definitions of the elements of financial statements (eg assets, liabilities, gains and losses);

4.   Recognition (When were the elements to be recognised in the accounts?);

5.   Measurement (How were the elements to be measured?);

6.   Presentation (How was the information to be presented to the user?); and

7.   The Reporting Entity (How should companies treat acquisitions of subsidiaries, mergers with other companies, joint ventures, associated companies and investments?).

In the UK, Professor David Solomons had prepared a report, 'Guidelines for Financial Reporting Standards' (1989), for the Research Board of the Institute of Chartered Accountants in England and Wales which attempted to set guidelines for the Accounting Standards Committee to aid it in setting standards. Solomons' Guidelines adopted a similar structure to those of the standard-setters and, indeed, went further than the others, on the question of measurement.

Given the virtual unanimity of view, the ASB decided to segment its own work similarly and consider each of the issues. The last five areas would affect specific standards. The first two however would affect the overall thrust of the Board's work. For that reason, one of the Board's earliest pronouncements (in July 1991) was an Exposure Draft 'The Objective of Financial Statements and the Qualitative Characteristics of Financial Information'.

Objectives and Qualitative Characteristics (Chapters 1 and 2)

The Board acknowledged (page 2) in the July 1991 Exposure Draft that much work had been undertaken on the principles underlying financial reporting - notably in the USA by the Financial Accounting Standards Board - but also by the three other standard-setters whose work had been considered by the Board. As the various published statements showed a large measure of agreement - any differences being limited to a matter of emphasis and drafting rather than matters of substance - the Board proposed to use the text of the 'Framework for the Preparation and Presentation of Financial Statements' published by the International Accounting Standards Committee (IASC) in 1989. In doing so the Board expressed its commitment to the IASC's work in promoting harmonisation in international accounting. The Board considered that for this initial exposure, it would be unproductive to add its own form of words where it agreed with the IASC and found that its statement adequately addressed issues relevant to the UK and the Republic of Ireland. Changes therefore from the IASC draft were minimal. In view of comments on the Exposure Draft, the Chapters were later re-written and reordered in the later omnibus Exposure Draft 'Statement of Principles for Financial Reporting' November 1995, which revised all seven previously issued chapters, but their essential thrust remained.

The two chapters were to be the guiding light for the ASB. The objectives of financial statements were deemed by the Board, like the other standard-setters, not only to be concerned with the traditional aim of stewardship but also "to provide information about the financial position, performance and financial adaptability of an enterprise that is useful to a wide range of users in making economic decisions". The informed investor was deemed to be the target of general purpose financial statements. In due course other reporting measures for less well informed users would have to be developed.

The main qualitative characteristics relating to content were deemed to be relevance and reliability and those relating to presentation were assessed as comparability and understandability. There is clearly a trade off between these characteristics. For example, a purchase cost of many years ago is reliable but is it still relevant today? Similarly, an estimate of value may be more relevant but is it too subjective to use?

On balance, the Board has come down in favour of relevance but not at the expense of total unreliability. Relevance, coupled with information for decision making, has led to a forward looking focus for financial reporting - the need to "tell it as it is" ie. what happened in the reporting period and then to describe its importance for the future. Consequently, in addition to the financial statements, narrative information, which would analyse and interpret the meaning of these statements, would be essential - the need for an analytical discussion by management such as an Operating and Financial Review now became clear.

The Board was reluctant to adopt the remaining chapters of the IASC framework as it believed that the chapters were not sufficiently detailed to be useful in the production of UK standards. This apparent deficiency was not surprising given that the International Accounting Standards Committee has a far wider constituency to satisfy than a national standard-setter and therefore is often unable to be as firm as it may wish on a particular proposal. Like all standard-setting bodies, the International Accounting Standards Committee has to muster enough votes to ensure the publication of any document!

The project directors responsible for the main standards on the Board's initial work programme were also assigned responsibility for the corresponding chapter in the Statement of Principles. This resulted in the remaining draft chapters of the Statement of Principles being published not in their eventual order within the overall Statement, but contemporaneously with their related Exposure Draft or standard. (See Appendix I)

Presentation (Chapter 6)

The first of the other chapters to be published in Exposure Draft form was Chapter 6 on 'Presentation of Financial Information' (December 1991) in tandem with FRED 1 'The Structure of Financial Statements - Reporting of Financial Performance'. Chapter 6 introduced the notion of the Statement of Total Recognised Gains and Losses. This had been derived from proposals in an earlier 1981 FASB Exposure Draft of Financial Accounting Concepts, 'Reporting Income, Cash Flows and Financial Position of Business Enterprises'[11] suggesting a move towards showing comprehensive income and from the notion of an additional performance statement proposed by the Institute of Chartered Accountants of Scotland (1988) in its seminal study 'Making Corporate Reports Valuable'. As FRED 1 stated (para 32):

"In assessing the overall financial performance of a reporting entity during a period, all changes in the net assets of a reporting entity arising from transactions or events, except those deriving from capital contributed by or payments to shareholders, need to be considered. The total of such changes is referred to as total recognised gains and losses."

The Statement of Total Recognised Gains and Losses initially merely sought to highlight what has become known as reserve accounting, reflecting changes in equity by adjusting reserves - in particular when dealing with revaluation gains or losses and changes in foreign equity investments financed by foreign currency borrowings, both of which were allowed by the Companies Act or by accounting standards to be taken to reserves. Given that the reporting of gains or losses on the revaluation of investment property portfolios is a critical feature of the accounts of investment property companies, it was perhaps surprising that this most important value change could be simply adjusted on reserves. The collapse of Polly Peck had also drawn attention to the problem of reserve accounting for foreign currency losses. In its 1991 accounts (note 25) losses of £44.7m on net investments overseas were taken to reserves. Profit before tax had amounted to £161.4m. In the preceding year, the losses on foreign investments had been even higher than profit before tax (£170.3m compared with £144.1m)[12]

While the notion of the Statement of Total Recognised Gains and Losses had been trailed prior to the issue of FRED 1 in a Discussion Draft entitled 'The Structure of Financial Statements - Reporting of Financial Performance' (1991), FRED 1 promoted the idea, and also took further, the notion expressed in the previously published Exposure Drafts of Chapter 1 of the Statement of Principles, for a need for information to be used for decision making. If information is to be used for decision-making, it is clearly important that users are able to distinguish income which will be continuing in the future and that which will have ceased. This led to the division of income into the continuing and discontinued elements originally introduced by the Accounting Principles Board in the USA (Opinion 30) in 1973[13]. There was a certain pressure on the Board to allow 'discontinuing' as opposed to 'discontinued' operations to be shown. The Board rejected these overtures because of the difficulty of determining which operations would be discontinuing and the suspicion that perhaps, so soon after the 1980's, a few companies at the margin might have been prepared to class loss-making businesses as discontinuing but have decided to retain them once profitability had improved!

A key, and controversial, feature of the FRED 1 proposals was the Board's determination to show gains and losses in the period in which they arose and not to show the same gains upon realisation in later years. (This approach is also a central feature of International Accounting Standard 16 'Property, Plant and Equipment'). For example, if an asset bought at 100 were revalued to 120, an unrealised gain of 20 would be displayed in the Statement of Total Recognised Gains and Losses in the year of revaluation and on disposal the gain or loss on sale shown in the profit and loss account would be calculated on the book value of 120, not on the original cost. It was recognised, of course, that many companies did not revalue assets and consequently those that had done so might believe themselves to be at a disadvantage in terms of the profit displayed on sale and, indeed, might well show lower operating profits given the increased depreciation charges on assets revalued above original cost. For this reason a note of historical cost profits was introduced to enable comparability to be obtained between companies that revalued assets and those that did not. Additionally, it would give the information traditionally regarded as essential for stewardship purposes. Interestingly, there has been little company or press comment about this note. Analysts still seem to look at the reported profit figure in the income statement rather than the historical cost profit reported in a note. It would seem there is not quite the interest in the traditional notions of historical cost income or stewardship as some would believe.

When the Board was debating the final drafts of what became FRS 3 'Reporting Financial Performance' (the standard based on FRED 1) the question of whether part of the gains on disposal on fixed assets should appear in the profit and loss account, given that unrealised gains appeared in the statement of recognised gains and losses, was debated at length. It was decided at that stage (mid-1992) that the latter statement should ideally show all changes (realised and unrealised) in the value of all fixed assets, not normally traded by the business but which were part of its infrastructure, leaving the profit and loss account to be more of a trading account. Such a dramatic change however would almost inevitably have meant re-exposure of the document and in view of the need to press on with the attack on other abuses then still prevalent, it was decided to postpone public debate of the issue. The Board's view that all gains on fixed assets should be taken to the Statement of Total Recognised Gains and Losses appeared in the revision to Chapter 6 in the full Exposure Draft of the Statement of Principles (November 1995).

Elements and Recognition (Chapters 3 and 4)

The key chapters of the Statement of Principles were those concerned with the definitions of assets, liabilities, gains and losses appearing in the financial statements, their recognition and their measurement (Chapters 3 to 5 respectively). The Board, in looking at some of the creative accounting techniques of the late 1980's, had identified in its work programme the need to eliminate off-balance sheet financing and to distinguish the difference between debt and equity. The Board had noted, with approval, the ASC's attempts to deal with off-balance sheet financing and, in particular, approved of its use of the IASC's definitions of assets and liabilities to determine when items should be shown on-balance sheet.

Internationally, standard-setters had produced very similar definitions of the elements of financial statements and consequently the choice of definitions involved relatively little discussion at Board meetings.

Assets were deemed to be "rights or other access to future economic benefits controlled by an entity as a result of past transactions or events" and liabilities were deemed to be "obligations of an entity to transfer economic benefits as a result of past transactions or events". Ownership interest would be the "residual amount found by deducting all of the entity's liabilities from all of the entity's assets". Gains and losses (which encompass both capital and revenue gains and losses) were deemed to be increases or decreases respectively in ownership interest other than those relating to contributions from or distributions to owners.

All these items were be recognised if:

(a)   there were "sufficient evidence that the change in assets or liabiliffes inherent in the element had occurred"; and

(b)   the element could be "measured at a monetary amount with sufficient reliability" - broadly meaning that different measurers of an item, using a measurement method that faithfully represented the quantity being measured, would arrive at amounts that were not materially different.

The Board used the definitions of assets and liabilities in developing Exposure Drafts which eventually became FRS 4 'Capital Instruments' (December 1993) and FRS 5 'Reporting the Substance of Transactions' (the off-balance sheet standard) (April 1994).

The problem tackled in FRS 4 was the tendency for companies to deem convertible instruments to be shares of a different nature. For example, some companies issued convertible, redeemable preference shares in a subsidiary but then accounted for the issue as if conversion to the ordinary shares of the parent company had already taken place - despite the fact the company could be obliged in certain circumstances to redeem the preference shares. At a premium. Another technique was the issue of capital bonds which had to be converted to preference shares at the end of their life these preference shares could then be redeemed. In this case it was argued that the debt was, in essence, a preference share since conversion had to take place[14]

The Board tackled these problems by means of its definition of a liability. In the case of the convertible, redeemable preference shares, the company had an <u>obligation</u> either to redeem the shares at the required price or to convert them at that value (the opportunity cost). In the latter case there would be a loss to the company since it had lost the opportunity to issue other shares at redemption (or a higher) value and had to accept the lower amount received earlier on issue for the existing shares. FRS 4 required the loss represented by the difference between the redemption price and the issue proceeds to be charged against profit over the period from the date of issue of the shares to the date of their redemption. Similarly, the capital bond still resulted in an obligation to pay interest until the date of conversion and consequently the Board decided that the bond was a debt.

FRS 5 sought to determine where the risks and rewards of a transaction lay. If the substance of a transaction was that a company was left with the risks and rewards of the rights to a future benefit, an asset had to be shown on-balance sheet. Similarly, if the company had an obligation to make a future payment, a liability had to be shown. Consequently, sale and compulsory repurchase transactions were no longer classified as sales but simply as loans. In substance, the "sale" proceeds were simply a loan secured against a demand to have the underlying asset repurchased by the company (in many cases the underlying assets never left the company's possession). Similarly, factoring transactions had to be examined to ensure that penalties for bad debts or slow payment risk did not fall on the seller of the debts. Only if the purchaser (the factor) accepted such risks could the debts be removed from the seller's balance sheet.

The definitions of assets and liabilities began to appear in other Board pronouncements. FRS 7 'Fair

Values in Acquisition Accounting' limited the ability of companies to establish provisions on the acquisition of another company. Previously, potential future trading losses and reorganisations after acquisition of a company had been deemed to be liabilities of the latter, thereby reducing its net worth and increasing goodwill. These provisions obviously enhanced post-acquisition group proffts. The Statement of Principles, however, indicated that future losses were not obligations. They could be avoided by the sale of the lossmaking business. Similarly, an intended reorganisation involved no commitment. While the acquirer's intention may have been to reorganise its acquisition, intentions could change and there was no obligation at present. Only if the acquired company had committed itself to this course of action and was unable realistically to withdraw from it would a liability be able to be recognised.

Similarly, the Discussion Paper on 'Provisions' (November 1995) prohibited what became known as "big bath" or "kitchen sink" provisions. Intentions to make huge reorganisations did not create a liability: therefore while the intention could be noted in the financial reports, a liability could not be booked.

These chapters of the Statement of Principles, therefore, created a new form of accounting. Accounting by management intent effectively was reduced if not eliminated. When criticisms were addressed to the Board claiming that the new proposals were not prudent, the Board responded by arguing that, while a huge provision may look prudent in the balance sheet, if there were no commitment for the expenditure to be made these provisions could be reversed in later years, flowing into income and creating artificially high income in future years. Consequently, prudence was only in terms of financial position. Such provisions sometimes were anything but prudent as far as the profit and loss account was concerned, depressing earnings in one year and over-stating them in future years.

The emphasis on assets and liabilities has led some critics of the Board's proposals to complain that the Board has rejected the matching concept. This is simply not true. As the Statement of Principles states:

"4.34 The process commonly referred to as 'matching' is, inter alia, a means of ensuring that where there is sufficient evidence that expenditure has resulted in access to future economic benefits, an asset is recorded until the period in which those benefits are consumed or expire at which time a loss is recognised. Matching means that expenditure directly associated with the generation of specific gains should be recognised as a loss in the same period as the gains are recognised, rather than in the period in which the expenditure is incurred. However, the application of the matching concept does not allow the recognition of items in the balance sheet that do not meet the definition of assets, liabilities or ownership interest.

4.35 When expenditure results in economic benefits that arise over several accounting periods and the association of the expenditure with the generation of specific gains can be only broadly or indirectly determined, and intermediate values of the asset cannot be directly obtained with sufficient reliability, it may be reasonable to assume that the asset declines in a systematic manner over its expected life. In these circumstances, an asset should be recognised and subsequently amortised on a systematic basis over the periods in which the benefits arise. This process forms part of the accepted methods of dealing with uncertainty. As noted above, perfect certainty of measurement is not required for recognition, and provided that this process results in a reasonable estimate of the asset and loss, they may be recognised on this basis. However, periodic reviews are required of the recorded amount of the asset to ensure there is sufficient evidence that future benefits of not less than this amount will occur."

Criticism of the Board has come in the form that the Board is concerned more with the balance sheet than the profit and loss account. Given the attention the Board has paid to performance statements in the revision of the profit and loss account (FRS 3), the introduction of the cash flow statement (FRS 1) and the Operating and Financial Review, this is difficult to accept. The Board does believe, however, that the balance sheet should show the resources at the company's disposal and the liabilities it is facing. It does not believe that the balance sheet should be used to hide unwanted debits and credits that management may not wish to take to income at the time they arise.

There are two ways to look at the role of the balance sheet. On the one hand, as the Board believes, a balance sheet can contain what people would normally deem to be liabilities and assets, ie. obligations and rights to the use of resources, or on the other, it can be deemed to be a residual statement containing deferred income and deferred costs. In most cases the results (if we ignore the valuation issue) would be similar but the second view enables certain debits and credits to be put in the balance sheet if they "distort income" and do not allow "proper matching". The Board found it impossible to operationalise terms such as the "non-distortion of income" and "proper matching". It believes that the performance statements should reflect all gains and losses when they arise and that such gains and losses should not be carried forward in the balance sheet. The Board would have difficulty in believing that a deferred loss was indeed an asset (the bigger the loss, the bigger the asset) or that deferred income was a liability. If, of course, income has been paid in advance and might have to be repaid, then there is a potential liability which should be displayed. If, however, income has just been shuffled from one year to the other, or losses such as start-up losses are carried forward and deemed to be an asset the Board would oppose the practices. See examples in Tweedie (1996).

In my view, performance statements ideally should "tell it as it is" ie show all the gains and losses of the year. The Operating and Financial Review should then explain these. As an example, consider the question of hedging future transactions. A company's profit is received in dollars. The dollar is expected to weaken against the pound in the next year and therefore the company hedges this potential currency loss by purchasing a dollar forward contract (covering next year's estimated dollar profits) expiring next year at today's dollar/pound rates. At the end of the year the forward is showing a gain as the dollar has started to weaken. Traditional practice is to ignore this gain and only recognise it when the forward contract expires and the gain is realised, yet the gain does exist and could be traded and realised at the period end. If the unrealised gain is recognised where should it be shown?

Some would argue it should be carried forward in the balance sheet (as a liability or as an unreported gain in ownership interest?) and "matched" against the future income. Nevertheless since the gain has arisen in the year in question, others would argue it should be shown in the performance statements and an explanation then given in the Operating and Financial Review that this identified gain is part of management strategy to mitigate a future fall in dollar values. In the following year the fall in profits could be explained in the Operating and Financial Review (or perhaps some additional performance statement) by reference to the currency gain of the previous year as follows:

	£m 19X1	£m 19X2
Total income of the year	55	45
Less gain on forward currency contract relating to future years trading	(5)	
Gain from forward currency contract of previous years relating to the current year	-	5
Total gain relating to the year	<u>50</u>	<u>50</u>

It is accepted that this is quite a change from present practice. To take the "record all gains and losses in the performance statement" proposal to its logical extent means that these statements will, in essence, become matters of record and the Operating and Financial Review (or a new statement) will become ever more important in the overall annual report, explaining _inter alia_ the overall trends of income resulting from management strategy by describing the currency gains obtained in one year to offset losses in a later year, thereby giving a longer term view of income. In other words, management would be telling the user of the financial statements how the business is operated in a strategic manner and lifting the user's eyes off the "bottom line", which has hitherto been deemed to encapsulate all that is important about a company's annual performance, to the longer term horizon. The alternative is to retain the present practice of adjusting income to reflect the underlying trend. A choice has still to be made!

Measurement (Chapter 5)

In its review of other conceptual frameworks, the Board was disappointed to find that no other standard-setter had considered in depth the controversial issue of measurement. Probably the trauma of the 1970's debates on inflation accounting weakened standard-setters' resolve in tackling the issue. The ASB, however, believed the issue had to be faced and, building on its earlier stated preference for displaying relevant information in financial statements, the Board quickly came to an opinion that current values were more relevant than historical cost.

Historical cost has the virtues of reliability and to a certain extent, objectivity (although allocations did mean a certain amount of discretion arose in determining an expired historical cost). Current values have the virtue of assisting users who wish to assess the current state of a company's net assets or its recent performance.

"A balance sheet containing assets and liabilities stated at current values reflects the current financial position of the business better than one containing such elements stated at historical costs. A profit and loss account and a statement of total recognised gains and losses prepared on a current value basis will give a better measurement of current performance than that provided by historical cost, in two respects. First, they will report the profits and gains that have occurred in the period rather than simply those that have been realised; secondly they will provide a fuller analysis of the reported profit by distinguishing profits generated by current

operations from gains resulting from changes in value while the assets were being held".
(Exposure Draft Statement of Principles for Financial Reporting, 1995, para 5.25)

Current value, however, is not without its disadvantages, the main one being its greater subjectivity and lower reliability than historical cost - particularly in the case of assets where there are not active markets and values have to be calculated. The Board expects, however, that as markets develop, objectivity and reliability will improve. A further problem with current values would be the lack of familiarity which would increase the cost of preparation. Nevertheless, independent research carried out in 1995 indicates that 60% of a sample of 510 listed companies revalued some operating properties (Company Reporting (1995)). Furthermore commodity dealers mark to market their stocks and investment companies show investments at market values (see ASB Discussion Paper, "The Role of Valuation in Financial Reporting', (1993), pp.24-27). There is therefore, a gradual trend towards current values.

The Board adopted, as its current value model, the deprival value system favoured in the Solomons Report (1989), whereby assets would be shown at their replacement cost or, if lower, their recoverable amount. (An adaptation of the old "cost or less" rule with which accountants are familiar.) The recoverable amount was deemed to be the higher of net realisable value or the value obtained from the asset's use and ultimate sale. The rule can be illustrated diagramatically.

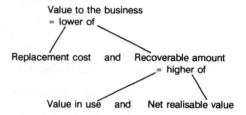

The deprival value system, in particular, the recoverable amount concept, was evident in the Board's proposals on goodwill (Working Paper, June 1995) and the Discussion Paper 'Impairment of Tangible Fixed Assets' (April 1996).

The ASB wished to ensure its intentions regarding its preference for current values were not mistaken.

> The Board stated (in the Exposure Draft Statement of Principles for Financial Reporting, 1995, para 6.42) "A balance sheet does not purport to show the value of a business enterprise. As a result of limitations stemming from reliability of measurement and costbenefit considerations, not all assets and not all liabilities are included in a balance sheet (eg some contingent liabilities are not included), and some assets and liabilities that are included may be affected by events, such as price changes or other increases or decreases in value through time, that are not recognised or are only partly recognised. Even if all recognised assts and liabilities were to be included at up-to-date values, the total of assets less the total of liabilities would not, except by coincidence, equal the value of the business. However, together with other financial statements and other information, balance sheets should provide information that is useful to those who wish to make their own assessments of the entity's value."

The Board was, also, cautious in proposing comprehensive use of current value given its disadvantages mentioned above. The Board is well aware of the danger of obliterating familiar landmarks by too swift a change in practice. It is for this reason that current cost accounting is unlikely to come on to the Board's agenda unless a high level of inflation and public demand forced the Board to consider the question. This gradual approach was reiterated in the Discussion Paper 'The Role of Valuation in Financial Reporting' issued in March 1993.

The responses to the Discussion Paper indicated that the Board's suggestion of a gradual move towards current values was supported. Out of the 64 respondents, only three proposed that there should be a return to historical cost. 45 supported a modified historical cost system with some values being shown, at current value, while four would have preferred a full-blown current value system. One respondent proposed that the Board should return to a current purchasing power accounting proposal similar to PSSAP 7 mentioned earlier[16].

The Board accepts the majority position and the current modified historical cost system will be with us for the foreseeable future although, in response to criticism, it is likely that the present system would be put on to a more consistent basis. In particular, the Board is debating whether to leave, as at present, the choice on valuation to companies but to require at a minimum that if certain fixed assets are revalued the whole class of those assets has to be revalued at the same time to avoid "cherry picking".

In addition, valuations would have to be kept up to date. This would remove the present problem whereby revalued assets are not written down when the market falls on the grounds that no permanent diminution had taken place. It is virtually impossible to audit whether something is "permanently" or "temporarily" diminished especially in volatile markets and consequently the Board does not intend to adopt a concept of permanent diminution. Instead the Board, in its valuation approach, would wish to reflect the market's present view of the future value of the asset.

The Reporting Entity (Chapter 7)

The final chapter of the Statement of Principles is concerned with the boundaries of the entity - ie. the extent of its control of assets and its related liabilities. Among the questions considered was how far these boundaries could be extended by investments in other companies. In many cases the investor's role is passive - it simply has invested for capital appreciation and annual dividend income. Other investments, however, are used to further the business of the investor and have consequences on the overall performance and financial position of the company and its group.

At one end is the controlled subsidiary, the resources of which are largely at the disposal of the investor (although the investor cannot disadvantage the other shareholders as a subsidiary's directors have to act in the interest of all shareholders). While, if a subsidiary were insolvent, an investor could in theory walk away without making good the subsidiary's net liabilities, in practice the actual damage that might be done to the investor means that in many cases, a liability of the subsidiary would be met by the investor unless it too was in serious financial difficulties. Given this situation, the practice has developed internationally of combining all the liabilities and assets of a subsidiary with those of the investor to show the overall group position, with the ownership interest of minority shareholders shown separately in the balance sheet and deducted in arriving at the net profit for the period.

Others have argued that only the share of assets and share of liabilities of the investor should be shown (proportional consolidation). The Board rejected this view as it believes that group accounts should be based on the notion of control and influence. In the case of a subsidiary, control is manifestly evident and proportional consolidation would not reveal the overall assets at the disposal of the investor. This was the basis that lay behind FRS 2 'Accounting for Subsidiary Undertakings', which was largely based on the 1989 Companies Act derived from the EC Seventh Directive, which in turn rests on the underlying notion of control.

In determining when a subsidiary existed, the Board also addressed the contentious issue of merger (pooling) v acquisition accounting. Under merger accounting, the merging companies are deemed to be one entity from the beginning of the accounting period. The assets are not revalued but simply added together and profit and loss accounts are combined for the whole year. Under acquisition accounting the acquired company's assets are revalued to fair value (reflecting the cost to the acquiring company of the acquisition of these assets). The excess of the purchase consideration over the fair value of the net assets is deemed to be goodwill. Profit of the acquired subsidiary is only included in the group profit and loss account from the date of acquisition.

Given the diversity of practice, the Board deemed it important to determine the principle under which a company could be deemed to have merged with or to have acquired another. The principle adopted was that used in Canada and latterly by the IASC, namely that merger accounting can only take place when an acquirer cannot be identified. Given that an acquirer can usually easily be identified, for example by the hostility of the takeover or the primacy of the management of the acquiring company, most business combinations are acquisitions. FRS 6 'Acquisitions and Mergers' (September 1994) introduced this principle in standard form, virtually eliminating pooling in the United Kingdom and the Republic Ireland.

The contentious issue of goodwill was also considered in the revision to the Statement of Principles. The Board had been criticised in responses to its Discussion Paper 'Goodwill and Intangible Assets' (December 1993) for not determining whether goodwill was an asset under the terms of the definition in Chapter 3 of the Statement of Principles. The Board accepted this criticism and in the November

1995 Exposure Draft of the Statement of Principles determined that goodwill was a bridge between the underlying investment shown in the balance sheet of the acquirer and the break-up of that investment into the assets and liabilities included in the group accounts. This led the Board to its view that neither arbitrary depreciation of goodwill on the grounds that it was similar to an asset, nor its elimination against reserves reflected the underlying value of the investment, and therefore an impairment approach of writing down goodwill only when the underlying investment lost value should be adopted[16].

Of course, not all major investments are subsidiaries. There is an intermediate investment in which the investor has no control, yet towards which it is far from passive: the investor uses the investment as a medium through which it conducts part of its activities. Unlike subsidiaries, these investments do not operate directly as extensions to dhe investor's business because the investor lacks control. Instead, special relationships exist of influence or joint control. In the case of an associated company, an investor would be interested in a long-term involvement through a relationship with the associate's directors and would exert significant influence over the operating and financial policies of its associate in the areas of concern to itself. The investor would, therefore, have a direct interest in the results generated by its investee and these are therefore reflected in its own performance statements.

Under SSAP 1 'Accounting for associated companies', a habit had developed of bringing into the investor's accounts its share of its investee's results, as determined by the proportion of equity capital it owned without enquiring too closely whether significant influence was exercised. While SSAP 1 requires significant influence to be demonstrated, such influence had not been defined in any great detail and, on some occasions, when the standard's 20 per cent threshold for identification of a possible associated company had been crossed, an investor automatically included the relevant proportion of the investee's profits in its own profit and loss account even if there was little contact between the two companies. In the latter situation the investment, though large, was essentially a passive one. It was unlikely, therefore, that any profit shown in the investor's profit and loss account reflected eventual cash flows attributable to the investor and, consequently, the Board in FRED 11 'Associates and Joint Ventures' (March 1996) de-emphasised the previous 20 per cent threshold and placed the importance on the concept of significant influence.

As far as joint ventures are concerned, the investor's relationship is not so much with the Board of Directors of a company as with its fellow investors. In this situation there is often joint control and where this exists the Board proposed that, once more, the investor's share of the investee's profits or loss, and not merely any cash withdrawn, would be included in its own performance statements. Ultimately profits of joint ventures would almost certainly be withdrawn and divided among the venturers.

4. Conclusions

The ASB's conceptual framework is, as we have discussed above, very similar to those existing in other countries. Common frameworks undoubtedly assist in the harmonisation of accounting and led to the formation of what has become known as the G4+1 group[17] standard-setters to work on common problems. Our ability to work together lies in the fact that we are all basing our thinking on similar concepts leading to the production of joint papers dealing with future events, hedging, provisioning and leases. The papers on hedging and leases dealt with issues where practice, though accepted for many years, was considered unsatisfactory by the standard-setters. The papers on future events and provisioning dealt with one of the major issues in accounting, determining to what extent the future should be brought into the present and, in particular, which future costs should be provided in the current year. It was in dealing with issues such as these that the importance of the definitions of the elements of financial statements become obvious.

As discussed above, the overseas conceptual frameworks had a major impact on the formulation of the new British and Irish accounting standards, which in turn have mirrored developments overseas and, in some cases, advanced international practice, taking advantage of new thinking based on the underlying principles.

It should be stressed that not all standards will be based on the Statement of Principles. In some cases adherence to the Principles would result in too dramatic a change to be presently acceptable. The Board has always maintained that it intends to proceed by evolution rather than revolution and in cases where it does not adhere to its own principles, it will explain that fact and state what it believes may be the ultimate solution. In this way the Board hopes to ensure the UK financial community thinks about new developments and perhaps, in time, may come to accept a more radical solution than that proposed in a new standard. It should be stressed, too, that the Statement of Principles will evolve. From time to time it will become clear that the principles have become outdated or may even have been incorrect as work on a new accounting standard reveals deficiencies in the existing text. In such cases the principles will, eventually, have to be changed in the light of experience.

Accounting is very much an evolutionary subject, changing with the sentiment of the financial community and with the emergence of new transactions or financial instruments. While, to some, the present Statement of Principles may look quite radical, it is almost certain that in 30 year's time, accountants will wonder how their counterparts of the 1990s could manage with such primitive underpinnings for financial reporting and will agitate for change. They will probably meet resistance to their proposals similar to that faced by the ASB in the 1990s!

Appendix 1

Relationship between the Board's work programme

and the Statement of Principles - publication dates

Statement of Principles	Substantive Issues
Chapter 6 'Presentation of Financial Information', Discussion Draft, April 1991 (superseded by Exposure Draft, December 1991)	The Structure of Financial Statements - Reporting of Financial Performance, Discussion Draft, April 1991 (superseded by FRED 1 and FRS 3)
Chapters 1 & 2 'The Objective of Financial Statements & Qualitative Characteristics of Financial Information', Exposure Draft, July 1991	
Chapter 3 'The Elements of Financial Statements', Discussion Draft, July 1992	Accounting for Capital Instruments, Discussion Paper, December 1991, (superseded by FRED 3 and FRS 4)
	Reporting the Substance of Transactions, FRED 4, February 1993 (superseded by FRS 5)
	Fair Values in Acquisition Accounting, Discussion Paper, April 1993 (superseded by FRED 7 and FRS 7)
	Accounting for Tax, Discussion Paper, March 1995
	Pension Costs in the Employer's Financial Statements, Discussion Paper, June 1995
	Provisions, Discussion Paper, November 1995
Chapter 4 'The Recognition of Items in Financial Statements', Discussion Draft, July 1992	The Role of Valuation in Financial Reporting, Discussion Paper, March 1993
Chapter 5 'Measurement in Financial Statements', Discussion Draft, March 1993	The Role of Valuation in Financial Reporting, Discussion Paper, March 1993
	Goodwill and Intangible Assets, Working Paper, June 1995
	Impairment of Tangible Fixed Assets, Discussion Paper, April 1996
Chapter 7 'The Reporting Entity', Discussion Draft, July 1994	Acquisitions and Mergers, FRED 6, May 1993 (superseded by FRS 6)
	Associates and Joint Ventures, Discussion Paper, July 1994 (superseded by FRED 11)
	Goodwill and Intangible Assets, Working Paper, June 1995

Note: While, in certain cases, the proposal to deal with a substantive issue was published before the relevant Chapter of the statement of Principles a draft of the latter would almost certainly have influenced the published paper.

References

Accounting Standards Board, Exposure Draft, The Statement of Principles, Chapters 1 and 2, 'The Objective of Financial Statements and Qualitative Characteristics of Financial Information', July 1991

Accounting Standards Board, Discussion Draft, The Statement of Principles, Chapter 3, The Elements of Financial Statements', July 1992

Accounting Standards Board, Discussion Draft, Statement of Principles, Chapter 4, 'The Recognition of Items in Financial Statements', July 1992

Accounting Standards Board, Discussion Draft, Statement of Principles, Chapter 5, 'Measurement in Financial Statements', March 1993

Accounting Standards Board, Discussion Draft, Statement of Principles, Chapter 6, 'Presentation of Financial Information', April 1991

Accounting Standards Board, Exposure Draft, Statement of Principles, Chapter 6, 'Presentation of Financial Information', December 1991

Accounting Standards Board, Discussion Draft, Statement of Principles, Chapter 7, 'The Reporting Entity', July 1994

Accounting Standards Board, Exposure Draft, 'Statement of Principles for Financial Reporting', November 1995

M Arden, 'The True and Fair Requirement', Foreword to Accounting Standards. ASB, 1993

Company Reporting No. 64, October 1995

R Dearing, The Making of Accounting Standards Report of the Review Committee under the Chairmanship of Sir Ron Dearing CB, ICAEW, 1988

L Hoffman & M Arden, Counsel's opinion on 'true and fair' ICAEW, 1983

ICAS, P McMonnies (Ed), Making Corporate Reports Valuable Kogan Page, 1988

A K Shah 'Creative Compliance in Financial Reporting', Accounting, Organisations and Society, Vol.21, No. 1, pp 23-39,1996

D Solomons, Guidelines for Financial Reporting Standards. ICAEW, 1989

D Tweedie and G Whittington, The Debate on Inflation Accounting, Cambridge University Press, 1984.

D Tweedie 'The Explicit Conceptual Frameworks Compared' IASC News. October 1991

D Tweedie, 'Regulating Change - The Role of the Conceptual Statement in Standard Setting', Edited by I Lapsley & F Mitchell, Accounting and Performance Measurement. Paul Chapman Publishing, 1996

Notes:

1. See Shah (1996).

2. 46% of the members of the ICAEW voted on the motion, "that the members of the Institute of Chartered Accountants in England and Wales do not wish any system of Current Cost Accounting to be made compulsory". The motion was carried by 15,512 votes to 13,184.

3. For further discussion on this issue see Tweedie & Whittington (1984) pp.74-137.

4. Many of these new pronouncements causing "the overload" were in fact products of the new Auditing Practices Board and the Cadbury Committee. At the instigation of the Financial Reporting Council, (the overarching body acting as trustees of the Accounting Standards Board and the Financial Reporting Review Panel), the ASB and the other bodies began to schedule their publication dates to avoid the simultaneous release of major pronouncements requiring comment.

5. The proposals appeared to be somewhat weaker when they appeared in SFAC 5 Recognition and Measurement in Financial Statements of Business Enterprises, 1984.

6. A particular problem with Polly Peck was that the profit and loss account reflected a highly inflationary nominal rather than a real profit. This issue was dealt with by UITF 9 'Accounting for operations in hyper-inflationary economies'.

7. This proposal had also been included in the ASB's Discussion Draft.

8. See Shah (1996) for a detailed discussion of these issues.

9. The remainder of the respondents did not express an opinion on the overall measurement techniques but commented on specific issues.

10. In practice, however, it is unlikely that a pure impairment approach would comply with company law.

11. The national standard-setters of Australia, Canada, the United Kingdom and the United States plus the IASC.

THE ROLE AND FUTURE PLANS OF THE INTERNATIONAL ACCOUNTING STANDARDS COMMITTEE

Sir Bryan Carsberg

There can be few who work for multinational companies, with some involvement with their financial reporting systems, who have not thought how good it would be to have one accounting language throughout the world. At present, accounting is far from that objective. Accountants inhabit a kind of Tower of Babel where we not only speak different languages but also give different interpretations of the same events and transactions.

The Need for Harmonisation

The desirability of uniform accounting has been apparent throughout the lifetimes of people who are alive today. However, only in the last twenty years or so has the case for it become compelling and only more recently have the pressures for uniformity become irresistible. One factor has been the increasing globalisation of business. Multinational companies have been with us for a long time. But economic trends are bringing more and more incentives to encourage genuinely international operation. The successful completion of the Uruguay round of GATT, leading to the establishment of the World Trade Organisation, will at least maintain the pace of change. Developments in the European Union are another important factor. As new countries join the Union and as companies adapt their businesses to become European companies, rather than companies of one nation, more and more multinationals are created.

Linked with this is the increasingly global nature of capital markets. If businesses are multinational in scope, it is likely that they will wish and need to raise their capital in many different countries. They are assisted in this by increasing competition among the capital markets, each anxious to increase its share of world business. Indeed, competition among the capital markets may be the strongest factor in encouraging a change of attitude by national regulators towards International Accounting Standards. The strongest capital markets of the world see the ability to accept International Accounting Standards as enabling them to compete more effectively: the need to prepare extra accounts to have a cross-border about the desirability of allowing domestic companies to use international standards for domestic purposes. They are concerned that otherwise domestic companies may be content with stock exchange quotations in other countries and see no need for a quotation on the domestic exchange.

The privatisation movement has also played a role in these developments. The transfer of utilities from state ownership to private ownership in many countries of the world, over the last ten years or so, has created new demands for private sector capital. The size of these demands is often too great to be accommodated in the capital markets of one nation.

Given the trends towards greater globalisation, the motivations of companies for seeking a uniform accounting system are strong. At one level, the motivation is to achieve economic operation. If companies have to prepare their accounts according to several different sets of rules, in order to communicate with investors in the various capital markets in which they operate, or for other national purposes, they incur a considerable cost penalty, and feel that money is wasted according to the standards of a rational world. However, the motivation goes deeper than this. Managers want to achieve as much congruence as possible between internal reporting and external reporting: only then can the incentives for good performance internally be linked faithfully to the measure by which the company will be judged in the outside world. Evidently, if different accounting rules have to be used to satisfy external requirements in different countries, a good match between internal and external reporting will be out of reach.

However, the case for uniform accounting goes much deeper still. The issue is fundamentally about the credibility of accounting. If a company reports dramatically different results for its operations, for a given year, because it has to publish results according to the rules in different countries, confidence in accounting will suffer. The well-known case of the results of Daimler Benz provides a dramatic example. In 1994, its reported profit under German rules was DM 895 million, whereas its profit under US accounting rules was DM 1,052 million. This is perhaps a relatively small difference, though not immaterial, and is in the direction that people have come to expect. German accounting rules are regarded as being more conservative some would say more prudent - so that profit measurements are likely to run lower than those made under US rules. However, it was the 1993 results which bade to write a new chapter in accounting text books. In that year, accounting under German rules showed a profit of DM 615 million; but US accounting led to the reporting of a loss of DM 1,839 million. How can accounting anywhere expect to be taken seriously when things like this can happen? Daimler Benz does not provide the only example of this kind of thing. The Norwegian company, Norsk Hydro, reported a profit of NKR 167 million under Norwegian rules in 1992 but a profit of NKR 1,763 million under US rules. News Corporation, an Australian company, reported a profit of A$502 million under Australian rules against a profit of A$241 million under US rules, also for 1992. The case of News Corporation, showing a difference of over 100% from US accounting to Australian accounting is particularly telling because people have tended to assume that differences of this kind arise only in contrasts between the rules of English-speaking countries and the rule of others.

National Differences in Accounting

People who study the differences among systems of accounting rules are inclined to group countries into two categories. On the one hand, there are countries where business finance is provided more by loans than by equity capital, where accounting rules are dominated by taxation considerations and where legal systems customarily incorporate codes with detailed rules for matters such as accounting. The effect of the taxation systems can be particularly pervasive. Often, the taxation systems effectively offer tax breaks for business by allowing a generous measurement of expenses and modest measurements of revenues, but on condition that these measurements are used for general reporting purposes. Companies have strong incentives to take advantage of these taxation concessions because real cash is involved. But the penalty is a lack of full transparency for arm's length equity investors in the businesses. In these countries, in the past, major providers of finance have been close to the companies in which they have invested, with private contractual arrangements to deal with the provision of information and perhaps involvement in management. The lack of transparency in the general accounts has not mattered so much. However, modern business pressures are changing this. The size of the capital needs, the wish to hedge finance-raising with operations or perhaps just a general wish to diversify have created reasons for companies to raise their capital in many different countries according to different customs. Major countries in this category include France, Germany and Japan.

The other group of countries is one in which equity sources of finance are more important, accounting measurements are not dominated by taxation considerations, because tax breaks can be enjoyed independently of the way results are reported to shareholders, and common law systems prevail. These countries generally have some private sector system for setting accounting standards, often within a general statutory framework. The role of equity finance is important because capital market pressures are then brought to bear most strongly to improve the quality of information available to investors: the absence of detailed codes, crystallised in the law, leaves flexibility to respond to pressures. The United States, the United Kingdom, Australia and the Netherlands are examples of countries in this category. The differences between accounting systems in the two groups of countries are often characterised as differences grounded in culture. This can be a troublesome description because it might be taken to imply that different accounting systems are needed from country to country. I am doubtful about that view. I believe the differences are more properly regarded as attributable to historical accidents, albeit accidents that have had a long-lasting effect because they have resulted in different ways of doing business. But pressures on accounting are changing as globalisation affects the way in which companies do business: it is not reasonable to suppose that German people are different from British people in ways that make them need different sets of accounting rules.

At this point, it is worth noting that no one nation has a set of accounting rules which appear to have such clear merits that they deserve adoption by the whole world. No one country can claim to have an uniquely correct set of rules. The United States has the longest history of standard setting. It has the largest standard setting organisation which is characterised by high standards of professionalism. But even the rules of the United States exhibit compromises between different interests of a kind which could reasonably have been decided differently. And no unanimity exists among US accountants about the merits of the precise details of the compromises that have been struck. One has only to look at US rules for an area such as accounting for pension costs to realise the force of this point. No one nation has a clear right, on the basis of existing achievements, to be regarded as predominant in accounting. A great deal more work is needed by accountants from different countries before we can reach the point of having a well-founded basis for uniformity and this work can take place, effectively, only at the international level.

The Founding of IASC

The next section of this paper gives some information about the history, composition and procedures of IASC to provide a basis for the final section which will set out our plans for the future. The development of accounting rules has a lengthy history in many countries of the world. The pace of development has varied from country to country, partly as a result of stimuli from economic events which affected nations differently. In the United States, for example, the traumas of the great Depression and the stock market crash, which brought to light a number of accounting scandals in the late 1920s and early 1930s, encouraged attention to some accounting issues as part of the subsequent reconstruction. A more recent wave of concern about some highly publicised cases, which caused people to conclude that accounting reports suffered from serious deficiencies, arose in the 1960s. A leading case in the United Kingdom involved a take-over in which the target company prepared a profit forecast as part of its defence. The take-over was successful and the actual report became available for the period for which the forecast had been made. It was dramatically different. More seriously, from the point of view of accounting, the subsequent investigation revealed that the differences were more attributable to the use of different accounting methods than to forecasting errors. This case and others of a similar kind provided the impetus for the establishment of formal procedures for setting accounting standards in the UK and Ireland.

However, a number of far-sighted accountants took the view that the problems of accounting should really be solved at the international level rather than the national level in order to achieve global uniformity. A start had been made with the formation of the Accountants' International Study Group in 1966, a co-operative venture of the professions in the United States, the United Kingdom and Canada. By 1972, the time was seen to be ripe for another step. At the 1972 World Congress of Accountants, held in Sydney, an agreement was made to establish the International Accounting Standards Committee and it commenced operations in 1973. Coincidentally, feeling in the United States had been growing in conviction that new institutions and approaches were needed to deal with difficult and long-running accounting issues in that country. In the same year as that in which IASC commenced operations, the US Financial Accounting Standards Board was formed to take over the setting of accounting standards from the Accounting Principles Board.

IASC was originally established as an independent organisation, the members of which were those professional bodies which were parties to the original agreement. It is still independent as far as decision-making is concerned: standards are approved by the Board of IASC and are not subject to confirmation by any other body. However, in 1983, IASC joined forces with the International Federation of Accountants (IFAC). The effect of this arrangement was that the members of IFAC became the members of IASC. These members are the professional accounting bodies from around the world, in round numbers about 110 professional bodies from about 85 different countries. IFAC now appoints the members of the IASC Board in consultation with the Executive Committee of IASC and it is also for IFAC to approve the IASC Constitution.

At the present time, the IASC Board comprises up to 13 country members and up to 4 additional co-opted members. Each member is represented by two individuals with a technical adviser if they wish to have one. IASC encourages variety of background in the individuals who represent Board members. We like, in addition to people in public accounting practice, to have people working in industry and in the user community on the Board. Academic accountants also have an important contribution to make.

The present Board members are: three from America: the United States, Canada and Mexico; five from Europe: France, Germany, the Netherlands, the Nordic Federation and the United Kingdom with Ireland; three from Asia: India, Japan and Malaysia; and South Africa and Australia. Four of the Board seats are "multinational". The United Kingdom has worked with Ireland in setting accounting standards since the process of setting standards commenced. The seat held by the Nordic Federation represents the Scandinavian countries who work together in a number of areas because of their geographic and economic affinity. In addition, an innovation introduced in July 1995 has involved the sharing of a seat between two countries in a more structured way. Sri Lanka has been included with India in its Board seat and Zimbabwe has been included in the seat occupied by South Africa. The co-opted places on the Board are seen as being useful in enabling it to widen the constituencies represented by including associations, preferably international associations, which have a good contribution to make and a real interest. The Board has three co-opted members at present. The first to join was the International

Co-ordinating Committee of Financial Analysts Associations, representing users of financial reports; and in the last year two organisations representing preparers have joined, the Federation of Swiss Industrial Holding Companies and the International Association of Financial Executives Institutes.

IASC is aware that the present size of its Board limits its ability to accommodate all the countries which have an interest in involvement in standard setting, particularly in the light of the expectation that a number of important nations may become able and willing to play a role in the future. The size of the Board is limited by the need to be able to have effective debate about technically complex issues. No doubt, a way will have to be found before long of involving more countries in our affairs but this may involve far-reaching questions about our organisation and procedures and the present Board will not wish to rush into decisions. A question which naturally occurs to people who consider the structure of IASC is whether or not it would be desirable that seats on the Board should be occupied by the national standard setters rather than the professional accounting bodies as happens at present. Some national standard setters would have difficulty under the present constitution and due process requirements in exercising a vote on the Board on behalf of their organisation. However, good communications between IASC and national standard setters are evidently important. We have welcomed the appointment of Sir David Tweedie, the Chairman of the UK Accounting Standards Board, as one of the UK Board members, and some other country members include members of their national standard setting boards in their representation. The US Financial Accounting Standards Board has a seat on the IASC Board as an observer member - that is, it does not vote - and a similar position is occupied by the Commission of the European Union. IOSCO, the international organisation of the securities regulators, has just been appointed to become a third observer member to improve communications in relation to our work programme in the context of the information I give below. Consideration is also being given currently to the question of whether other countries which may become strong members of the international economy in the future should be introduced to a relationship with IASC through observer membership of the Board.

Due Process

IASC develops its standards in accordance with procedural rules. A steering committee is formed to develop proposals for each technical matter on the Board's agenda. The steering committee is usually chaired by a member of the Board and it works with a project manager from the IASC staff to agree on the research required and prepare draft documents. The steering committee publishes a draft Statement of Principles for public comment on its main project. This is the basis for the Board's settling a Statement of Principles, which is published, and subsequently an Exposure Draft which is made available for public comment. Exposure Drafts must be approved for publication by two thirds of Board members and finalised Standards must be approved by three quarters of Board members. This means that we face the demanding challenge of obtaining twelve positive votes for a Standard out of the present Board membership of sixteen. The Board normally meets three times each year, and with the possibility of a fourth meeting where needed, the procedures required for agreeing a Standard can be completed in the most favourable circumstances in about two years.

IASC's Achievements

This paper next comments on some of the achievements of the Board in its twenty-two years of life. Originally, the objective of the Board was to produce "basic standards". This, no doubt, reflected the view that it would be easier to reach agreement on basic standards than on highly detailed standards and it addressed the wish to have standards that would be readily usable in developing countries as well as improving the level of hammonisation among the richer countries of the world. Early standards often allowed alternative treatments to accommodate the different approaches adopted by national standards setters.

Today we give importance to providing standards that will bring greater uniformity to accounting reports of multinational companies, particularly those with stock market quotations, but we continue also to wish to have our standards used in developing countries. A number of countries, some relatively wealthy and others relatively poor, take international standards as the basis for local standards, issuing them locally with little or no amendment. However, the idea that we could restrict our standards to basic matters has long since been abandoned. As the world develops more and more complex contractual arrangements, including financial instruments, genuine uniformity in global accounting calls for more extensive and sophisticated standards.

IASC has also recognised the need to reduce alternatives wherever possible. Allowing alternatives can work against real harmonisation. Their elimination can cause pain to businesses which have become accustomed to the flexibility provided by alternative treatments but the LASC Board has been able to make a good deal of progress in eliminating alternatives, particularly in its omnibus project on Improvements and Comparability, completed in 1993. IASC has just issued its 32nd statement of International Accounting Standards. It also has a framework document which deals with the objectives of financial reporting and definitions of the qualities required in financial reporting and the elements of financial statements. Its framework document is similar to corresponding statements of the national standard setters.

An organisation like IASC must give a good deal of attention to the means by which it encourages use of its pronouncements. An international organisation of its type cannot expect to have direct legal backing and it must look for other means. The Member Bodies of IASC undertake to promote the use of international standards in the countries where they operate. Recommendations of professional accounting bodies can be highly influential and this is particularly the case when international standards are converted into local standards whether or not they have the force of law.

The IOSCO Agreement

Acceptance of international standards for financial reporting connected with stock exchange listings is another important way for IASC to make progress. Our standards are already accepted by several stock exchanges, the London Stock Exchange having led the way soon after the foundation of IASC. However, the regulatory arrangements in some key countries still do not permit the use of international standards for stock exchange purposes and North America and Japan are prominent among these. IASC has therefore been holding discussions with the International Organization of Securities Commissions (IOSCO) to explore the possibility that IOSCO would endorse our standards and thereby give some additional impetus to movements towards acceptance in stock exchanges.

The past Chairman of IASC, Eiichi Shiratori from Japan, pressed strongly for IOSCO endorsement of our standards as they stood at the time. However, some members of IOSCO took the view that endorsement should be withheld until we had completed a core set of standards, a set which dealt comprehensively with the main financial reporting issues of the day. In 1995, IASC decided to accept the need to complete a core set of standards before endorsement could be expected. Completion of this core set is a desirable objective for IASC in any event and acceptance of this objective enabled us to make a good agreement with IOSCO, in which we both undertook to co-operate in seeking to complete the core set of standards as effectively and quickly as possible, and in which IOSCO expressed warm support for our objectives. IASC and IOSCO published this agreement in July 1995. It focused on a work programme which would be completed in mid-1999 and which covered all the areas which IOSCO saw as needing attention for IASC to have completed its core set of standards. The agreement with IOSCO says that the completion of the work programme will clear the way for IOSCO endorsement of our standards. IASC took pleasure in promoting this work programme as a plan for this millennium.

During the first few weeks of 1996, several of the key members of IOSCO asked IASC to consider accelerating its work programme. The need for a body of standards that can be used universally in cross-border offerings and listings is urgent. Companies wishing to raise capital on international stock markets in the near future would want to do so without incurring the costs of preparing a new set of accounts and without delay. The capital markets wanted to enjoy the benefits of removing some of the friction affecting their competition. So IASC reassessed its work programme and at the March 1996 Board meeting agreed to adopt fast track procedures which could lead to completion of the core set of standards by March 1998. The precise decision of the Board was that fast track procedures should be adopted and that the staff should proceed with the accelerated work programme as resources permit. The new programme is given as an appendix to this paper.

The Current Work Programme

The work programme is tough and ambitious. It imposes a heavy burden on Board meetings in particular. It includes a list of sixteen projects, some of which are revisions of existing standards rather than the preparation of completely new ones, and it calls for the Board to discuss about seven substantial technical matters at each Board meeting over the next two and-a-half years. Several of the projects involve controversial subjects. The project on Income Taxes, the one which is nearest to completion, is one where the national standard setters of the world are far from being in agreement about the broad approach which should be adopted. The topic of financial instruments is one where no national standard setter has a comprehensive set of requirements in operation. The area of intangibles is linked to accounting for goodwill and controversies about these items continue to loom large in the world of financial reporting. Significant and difficult issues have to be dealt with in the projects on segments, non-wage employment costs, interim reporting, provisioning and leases. And this is not to suggest that any of the projects on the list will be completely straightforward. The project on agriculture is perhaps worthy of note for two reasons. One is that the project is being undertaken with the support of a major grant from the World Bank. The other is that it is not part of the IOSCO core requirements. Some of the other projects are likely to go beyond the issues identified by IOSCO as needing coverage in the core programme but the project on agricultural accounting is the only one on the list which is completely outside the IOSCO requirements.

The list of projects in the current IASC work programme does not, by any means, exhaust the projects for which some demand exists. In particular, we are experiencing increasing demand for development of standards to deal with specialised industry problems. Projects for insurance accounting and accounting for the extractive industries are high on the list of other projects for which demand exists. IASC would like to meet the needs of these specialised industries as soon as resources permit.

Another urgent area for us concerns the interpretation of International Accounting Standards. All standard setters find that their pronouncements often lead to detailed questions about application to specialised situations, sometimes involving minor extensions of the area covered by the central focus of a standard. IASC is no exception and staff already receive a number of requests for help with such matters which they deal with informally. However, as the role of International Accounting Standards grows, more difficulties may arise with aggressive interpretations of standards. For this and other reasons greater need is likely to be felt for help with interpretations and more weight will be given to the desirability of formal interpretations, backed by some form of due process. Some of the national standard setters have special procedures to deal with such needs and the IASC Executive Committee has decided that it should have similar special procedures. Lack of a procedure for interpretations by IASC might lead to the emergence of local procedures for interpretations and these might well detract from the degree of harmonisation achieved. IASC needs a procedure which is reasonably fast and inexpensive. The Executive Committee will be recommending the establishment of such a procedure at the June Board meeting. We may start work on issuing interpretations later this year, perhaps using an electronic due process. It is committed to introducing such a procedure as soon as resources permit.

IASC and Europe

Another body with which IASC has an important relationship is the Commission of the European Union. The EU has an important interest in international harmonisation of accounting, at least as far as the Sfteen member countries of the Union are concerned. One of the key objectives of the Union is to promote the development of the member countries into a single economic market, characterised by fair and effective competition. Use of a uniform accounting system is important for effective competition in the capital markets, because the markets are unlikely to be able to evaluate, on an even basis, companies which prepare their reports according to different sets of accounting rules. The interest in a harmonised system of accounting may also go deeper than this. Harmonised accounting may be important for even competition in the markets for goods and services and the application of competition law towards those markets.

The main vehicle for accounting harmonisation within the EU was initially the series of directives on company law. The Fourth Directive and the Seventh Directive are well-known for containing some key provisions about acceptable accounting methods. However these directives, being like statutes, are not suitable vehicles for the main task of setting accounting standards. Changing to existing directives and issuing new ones is a lengthy political process. Accounting rules in such directives become out of date and cannot easily be revised particularly because of the difficulties of the multinational political process involved. Something more flexible is needed. Early in 1995, a good deal of speculation was reported in the newspapers about the possibility that the European Commission would call for the establishment of a European accounting standards board. This possibility was of concern to most accountants. A European accounting standards board would be expensive and, given its need to start from scratch, it would be likely to take a long time in reaching agreement on a reasonable number of standards. Furthermore, harmonisation within the European Union would not be likely to be significantly easier than harmonisation on a worldwide basis. The differences in present approaches among such countries as Italy, Spain, France, Germany, the Netherlands and the United Kingdom are as great as any that exist on a global scale. Surely, many argued, it would be better to regard IASC as the most promising body for establishing accounting standards as a basis for harmonisation within the EU. In this way, advantage could be taken of the considerable progress already made. The European Commission already had a seat as an observer member of the IASC Board and it could certainly step up its contribution to deliberations in IASC.

Happily this is the line which the Commission has now decided to adopt. A speech by Mr Monti, the European Commissioner with responsibility for accounting policy, in a speech at the IOSCO conference in July 1995, put the idea of a European accounting standards board to rest. He said: "We would therefore welcome an agreement between IOSCO and IASC on the endorsement of a comprehensive set of International Accounting Standards. We believe that companies should only be required to prepare one set of consolidated accounts and we plan to examine the possibility for European companies with an international vocation to prepare their consolidated accounts on the basis of International Accounting Standards. We equally intend to strengthen the European input in the international accounting harmonisation debate. This is not an appeal for the creation of a European accounting standards board, nor is it our intention to create a new layer of European accounting standards on top of the existing layers (national standards and international standards). Improved co-ordination of the activities of our member states in the area of accounting standards-setting will allow us to operate more efficiently and will ultimately facilitate international harmonisation."

In mid November 1995, the European Commission released a communication on accounting harmonisation which clarified its intentions still further. It said that would ally itself more closely with the efforts being undertaken by IASC and IOSCO towards a broader international harmonisation of accounting standards. The communication was particularly notable for its recognition that only IASC is producing results which have a clear prospect of recognition within a time scale which corresponds to the urgency of the problem. The Commission said that, as a first priority, it would examine International Accounting Standards to establish whether there were any conflicts with the European Directives on accounting. Conflicts were not thought to be likely but the intention was that, if any were found, action would be considered to eliminate them. The Commission noted that the Directives gave member states certain options in incorporating the accounting directives into national law. Even if no conflicts exist between International Accounting Standards and the Directives, conflicts may exist with national laws because of the options chosen. The Commission said that it is up to member states to consider this issue and deal with it at the national level. The Commission would try to work more closely with IASC in the future and in particular would explore the possibility of reaching an agreed view among the representatives of member states on the Commission's "Contact Committee" about IASC Exposure Drafts for submission to IASC.

These encouraging developments in thinking in Brussels are matched by developments in France. In a public speech in September, the Minister of the French Government responsible for accounting matters said that he was proposing to introduce a new law in France strengthening the position of accounting standards. He proposed to strengthen the position of the procedures for setting French national accounting standards and, in a landmark development, to recognise international standards with a sufficiently broad level of authority for use by French companies. The probable effect is that International Accounting Standards will be able to be used by French companies for domestic purposes as well as cross-border purposes. The new law in France has been circulated privately in draft for comment and is likely to be introduced in Parliament in the near future.

Similarly encouraging developments are taking place in Germany. German companies increasingly are feeling the need to participate in international capital markets, to raise equity capital and serve existing and new shareholders more effectively. German companies, therefore, are increasingly feeling the need to use an international set of accounting standards. Movements in this direction have been inhibited by German requirements for conformity between the accounts which form the basis for taxation assessments and the accounts which report financial results to shareholders. Recently, German government officials have been signalling the possibility of a way out of such constraints. The conformity rule might be maintained for the accounts of individual companies while use of International Accounting Standards would be "tolerated" for the preparation of group accounts, the important accounts for reporting to shareholders. This might well be a way of avoiding the need to prepare more than one set of accounts for the purposes of operations in the capital markets. A further boost to IASC's standing in

Germany was given recently by the decision of Deutsche Bank to use International Accounting Standards in its financial reporting.

Resources

The ambitious programme facing IASC over the next four or five years requires us to seek an increase in our resources. In 1995, our expenditure for mainstream standard setting activities was about £1.2 million. In round numbers, £600,000 comes from contributions from Board members, £300,000 comes from other contributions, about half from the international accounting firms and half from businesses and otherss and about £300,000 comes from contributions earned on our publications. This budget compares with a budget of US $16 million for the US Financial Accounting Standards Board and about £2 million for the UK Accounting Standards Board. Some aspects of the work of IASC are particularly expensive as a result of our need to operate at a global level. Board meetings and meetings of steering committees are expensive because we have to pay the expenses of a number of people who come long distances to meet together. On the other hand, we also have some advantages. We are often able to use the fundamental research which has been undertaken by national standard setters and, like many standard setters, we are helped by volunteers who contribute their time free of payment.

We decided in mid 1995, in conjunction with the original IOSCO agreement, that we needed to increase our annual budget to about £1.75 million to be able to achieve our objectives effectively. The acceleration of the work programme to aim at completion in 1998 would be more expensive and would involve having a budget of about £2.3 million a year for the next two years. We have recently established a high level Advisory Council to help us with our funding needs and to advise us more generally. With the assistance of our Advisory Council, we are embarking on a programme to raise funds in various countries of the world. We shall seek a relatively large number of relatively small contributions but we shall ask those who agree to help us to agree to give us an annual sum for the next five years. We already obtain a sizeable amount of financial strength from the sale of our publications. This has been increasing steadily over the years and is likely to continue to do so as our standards become more comprehensive and as we move towards their acceptability for cross-border listings on stock exchanges.

We would like to be able to rely more on publication income over the longer term. However, our ability to reach the position enjoyed by the US Financial Accounting Standards Board, for example, where two thirds of its income comes from publications, is likely to take some time in coming. Dissemination of our standards often involves translations costs and we do not want to price our publications at a level which inhibits their use in the poorer countries of the world.

IASC and National Standard Setters

Completion of our work programme in 1998 and obtaining IOSCO's endorsement is our first objective. This is likely to secure general acceptability of International Accounting Standards for cross-border listings on stock exchanges. However, this is only a beginning for IASC. The main goal, the objective to which all our efforts must ultimately be directed, is to bring about complete unification of the world's accounting systems: uniformity between International Accounting Standards and the national standards of all countries. We need to work with national standard setters to achieve this goal. We do not see our activity as competitive with national standard setters. We rather want to join with them in the debate about the merits of alternative solutions, taking advantage of their special position in communicating with constituencies in their own countries, so that we can move together towards agreement on preferred solutions.

A system has grown up in recent years for facilitating this co-operation. Frequent and regular meetings of standard setters are now held. IASC participates in meetings of the so-called G4 + 1, the national standard setters of the United States, Canada, Australia and the United Kingdom and Ireland, together with IASC. Other meetings of standard setters take place in small or large groups. Through these consultative arrangements, we aim to co-ordinate agendas and we also aim to try to adopt common solutions. We cannot yet be sure of our ability to agree on all the key points but at least we must make sure that each of us considers the solutions which are congenial to our colleagues. Special opportunities for progress can be created by undertaking certain projects jointly. Our work on financial instruments, for example, has been undertaken jointly with the Canadian standard setters. And our work on earnings per share and reporting the results of segments involves close liaison with national standard setters.

People at IASC are sometimes pressed with a question about where all this work on harmonisation is leading to. The objective of one uniform system of accounting throughout the world is clear. No doubt it will take a good deal of time to get there. But what is the implication of this plan for the present structure of standard setting? Will there be room for several national standard setters in the world of the future or will the world have just one standard setter and will that one be IASC? This is an understandable question although asking it is a bit like asking whether we shall have world government one day. I do not think any of us at IASC are looking towards a time when there will be only one standard setter. The extent to which individual countries use our standards as national standards, or maintain their own procedures is a matter for decision at the national level. As far as IASC is concerned, a cooperative relationship with national standard setters provides the best prospect for progress. The details of that relationship may need to change. IASC may need to alter its own structure and, as part of that, find a way of closer and more formal incorporation of national standard setters into its decision-making process. Whatever the details of these changes, we shall continue to need the contribution of people who are well versed in local views about accounting and we need the help of the expertise of national standard setters more generally. Setting accounting standards is strangely complex and controversial. Good solutions are likely to come from the maintenance of several standard setting bodies who can contribute to the debate but who agree on the importance of international harmonisation.

KEEP RIGHT ON, TOWARDS CORRIGIBLE ACCOUNTING

John Perrin

Introduction

During the Great War Harry Lauder used to cheer the troops, including my own father, with a song which I believe included the lines "Keep right on to the end of the road, Keep right on to the end". Some readers may remember the other lines, which included words or phrases such as "weary", "dreary", "long" and "round the bend". Arguably this song could be adopted by accounting academics. And if one goes on 'round the bend' for long enough,one may come out more or less where one started. This, too is apt for the study of accounting.

Professor Will Baxter began his accounting teaching career nearly seventy years ago. I began my teaching forty-five years ago. By then there was a large literature (even if small compared to today), and with the optimism of youth I thought that Will Baxter and others had solved most of the fundamental problems of accounting. Henceforth the main challenge would be the implementation of the logic of good accounting, and working out how to apply this logic in practice. In other words, I assumed that accounting and accountancy were corrigible. Of course, now I realise this was naive, as was the implicit assumption that change in the environment of business, government and trade would not constantly require re-examination of all prescriptions for good accounting.

There was a very recent reminder of how situations at least partly repeat themselves, only with change of detail and progress of technology. It was announced that because of theft of flowers from a cemetery in Scotland, for reselling at 'boot sales' and elsewhere, the local police were offering a service of dye-marking the flowers to deter thieves through making detection on resale easier. This brought to mind the classic case of McKesson & Robbins (discussed inter alia by Kenneth MacNeal in Baxter & Davidson, 1962). Reputedly the Coster family had gained control of McKesson & Ribbins after amassing capital from the American (alcohol) prohibition period, with a sideline in recovering flowers from cemeteries at

85

night and selling them on as fresh flowers again the next day. The Coster flowers in the 1930s were real flowers, and could not be traced. Today's flowers are of artificial silk, can be obviously or secretly marked, and can be traced. Thus, the same basic problem, but new technologies. However, while the McKesson & Robbins' scandal of falsified stock inventories led to the American requirement that auditors must observe and sample annual stocktaking, it is not at all clear that the recent news from Scotland will have any direct impact on auditors, accountants, or the academic study of accounting. Other debacles and scandals will have much greater impact.

All roads used to lead to the LSE (London School of Economics). I was privileged to be there at a vibrant time: Will Baxter (mentor), Harold Edey (doctoral tutor), Ronald Edwards, Basil Yamey and David Solomons as external examiner. And in the evenings there were seminars with guests, such as the founders of the Forte and tugendhat entrepreneurial empires, most of whom admitted that their success had been in spite of, rather then because of, their ignorance of the formal intellectual theories of accounting and economics. The tycoons who came to the LSE forty years ago were very modest, even humble, or else they dissembled more successfully than do many of their modern counterparts.

This essay will move in three stages from the general to the particular. First there are some observations on the 'general case' of accounting, essentially the field of financial accounting and reporting for which Will Baxter published so much of importance and relevance. But this essayist, after early specialisation in industrial and management accounting, later redirected his research to the public sector. So the second stage of the essay will briefly consider a few issues in public sector accounting more generally, before moving to a final stage examining problems with public sector capital accounting, its measurement and disclosure, and the public accountability implications which follow therefrom. This latter stage links back to contributions which Professor Baxter has made to our concern and understanding for accounting for capital (assets), depreciation and the effects of inflation and other price-level changes. Inclusion here of all these topics may seem - and indeed is - superficial, but profound treatment would require a book-length manuscript.

Financial accounting is the mainstream: it distils a mixture of law, and of commercial and financial practice with a dash of economics added, into the particular if not peculiar mystique of 'accountancy'. In contrast, the narrow or strict definition of management accounting requires little of this mystique: it is mainly based on economic principles and understanding of the particular organisation, its operational characteristics (i.e. procurement, production, markets, etc.), and preferably its behavioural environment. Professor Baxter has contributed to both these branches of accounting, but arguably his greater contribution has been to financial accounting.

Academic accounting has increasingly diversified, partly through using accounting data, skills and concepts to explore a wide range of societal or managerial issues over and beyond the measurement and reporting of economic or financial performance of a specific host or client organisation, as was the original and dominant role in practice. There has been concern that diversification may have gone too far, or at least that academic accountants nowadays are not making the scale (or quality?) of contribution they should be making to real-world practising accountancy (see Whittington, 1995 and 1996). Professor Whittington has made a useful distinction between academic research on the 'content' and on the 'context' of accounting. I am tempted to suggest a further subdivision, for 'process', to include the intellectual and practical activities of devising and agreeing the content of accountancy, and its implementation into accepted practice, law or regulation.

Professor Will Baxter's interests have spanned content, context (including his work in accounting history), and process. This is demonstrable from his collected papers (1978), as from his selection of papers in the classic volume with Professor Davidson (1962). The earlier works in these publications reflect concern for the uneasy relationship between economics and accounting, accounting costs for pricing and other decision-making, problems of reform and authority in determining accounting concepts and principles, the interpretation of published accounting statements, and the impact of price level change on accounting measurement and reporting. The latter area, linked with depreciation accounting, became preoccupations in three of Baxter's later books (1971, 1975 and 1984). His approach to some of this work was very possibly strongly influenced by his early conversion to the importance of the balance sheet over other accounting statements, as revealed in the Preface to his collected papers (1978).

At least some of my generation, when students, thought that most of the truths and needs of accounting must have been discovered already, whether by Baxter or in the already extensive American academic and professional literature. But, carrying on round the bend of time, the wheel had to be reinvented, either because people forget earlier wisdom, or else because truths are not absolute, but change, along with needs, as the economic (and political) environments evolve. But some of us thought that when academics (such as Edward Stamp and Kenneth Peasnell) and practitioners were brought together to hammer out "The Corporate Report" (1975), that at last there would come about some more or less final agreement on financial reporting and the underlying accounting principles (except for price level/inflation accounting remaining unresolved).

"The Corporate Report" "sought to satisfy, as far as possible, the information needs of users" defined "as those having a reasonable right to information", and comprising "the equity investor group, the loan creditor group, the employee group, the analyst-adviser group, the business contact group, the government and the public". Currently, we could encompass these user-groups simply as the 'stakeholders'. But again in the spirit that very little is entirely new, I have a nagging feeling in the rearmost depths of memory that the term 'stakeholder' was in use in similar contexts in American accounting and management literature as much as half-a-century ago, possibly first by Chester Barnard.

"The Corporate Report" recognised that different user groups needed differing types, degrees and formats of information. It gave support to the idea of 'multi-column reporting' to meet differing user needs. But this idea was never taken up effectively by the accountancy profession, possibly because the idea implied some parity of esteem among different user groups, whereas the worlds of industry, finance and accountancy still wished the 'equity investor group' to have primacy. More prosaically, practitioners probably thought that users would be confused by multi-column reporting, reconciliation between columns would be difficult, and such full/multiple disclosure would weaken the mystique and image of accountancy being capable of generating the single and best most-true-and-fair judgement of accounting income and valuations.

More Recent Developments

"The Corporate Report" was produced under the auspices of the Accounting Standards Steering Committee (1975). A generation onwards, a newer body, the Accounting Standards Board, has produced a successor report, the "Statement of Principles for Financial Reporting" (Exposure Draft, 1995), doubtless much influenced by David Tweedie. This new statement is more detailed than the earlier report, and it may well prove more acceptable to the accountancy profession, yet without greatly alienating the academic accounting community. I wish to Godspeed, but I cannot help wondering if its essential truths will not have to be rediscovered and rephrased yet again after another generation, if not sooner. Presumably we just have to accept that there are no eternal scientific truths in accounting, or at least no ways of phrasing these to convey constant understanding and conviction in a changing world.

Management accounting, also, has moved forwards. There are sundry permutations of activity-based costing (ABC), and of systems for just-in-time and total quality management approaches. But some of these may be but old ideas repackaged with new jargon: accounting historians could usefully spend more time critically researching modern accounting history. Take ABC. I was recently sorting my old lecture notes from the early 1960s, and I discovered that I had been teaching 'transaction cost analysis' and its use for improved cost allocation. Using different labels, the notes contained much of the essence of modern ABC. Alas, my notes did not mention the source of these ideas, and I do not claim to have invented them. Yet here again is rediscovery of accounting ideas, although nowadays often also with commercial hype and promotion added on.

For most of the newer developments in accounting we have to look to the academics, and especially their work in Whittington's 'context' subject areas - social and critical accounting, and environmental accounting. One area new or renewed a generation ago, human capital or human resources accounting, seems to have received less attention recently. Accountants may have to be provoked from outside their own discipline to give proper attention in future to human and intellectual capital, as keystones to future economic success (Angell, 1995).

Creative accounting is not properly a new development, but only just a continuing, evolutionary development. Adam Smith would have recognised it, even if he would have given it another name, possibly as some distinctive type of 'conspiracy'. And as noted by Lee (1995), there are "doubts about the ability of accountants to resist managerial pressures to misreport". Some of these pressures may be to exaggerate income and growth, while the natural caution of accountants may lead them to desire 'flexible' accounting principles making it easier to achieve 'income smoothing'. In his review of the 83 readings in Zeff & Dharan (1994), Forker (1996) makes the point that "the central theme ... is the tension between accounting policy makers and preparers of financial statements ... attributed to the preferences of preparers for flexibility in the application of accounting conventions, primarily to facilitate the objective of smoothing income". Of course, smoothing income is not inherently evil: but it does usually involve judgements, about the future regarding which the accountant has little expertise, as well as about the past which has been his traditional province.

One antidote to creative accounting is the prominent reporting of cash flow accounting, whether in multi-column format or otherwise. Both T A Lee and G H Lawson (see in Bromwich & Hopwood, 1981) have done much to promote cash flow accounting intellectually, and perhaps now FRS 8 will bring more rigour to cash flow accounting in practice. It might seem paradoxical at the same period in time, that cash flow accounting in the public sector is being downgraded in favour of accrual accounting. Cash flow accounting may be the less true and fair, but it is probably also less open to creative accounting abuses.

Nowadays, to assist navigation between the Scylla of inadequate accounting and the Charybdis of excessively creative accounting, we have 'Generally Accepted Accounting Practice in the United Kingdom' (UK GAAP, 1994). My edition runs to 1610 pages. Uniform accounting might not require such a lengthy manual. GAAP accounting and financial reporting is a creature particular to the Anglo-American business cultures. If the Anglo-American business hegemony declines much further, we may see international preference swing more towards uniform accounting and reporting. This need not be seen as the end of civilisation. It could be done in a multi-column format, with a column (and notes and schedules) to report also the creative accounting alternative. Meanwhile it is a case of heeding the familiar London cry, "Mind the GAPP".

The gap more usually discussed is the 'audit expectations gap', whereby it is argued that auditors fail to deliver the information or the conviction needed, or at least 'expected', by users of published accounts. More recently it is being argued that the audit expectations gap is really only a symptom of a more fundamental problem, a 'financial reporting expectations gap'. The latter might be curable only by some combination of reforms which could include increasing the independence of auditors, at the extreme by removing their selection and appointment from the control of company directors; or moving towards standardised multi-column or even uniform reporting. Tom Lee (1995) has written interestingly on some of these, and other, issues facing the future credibility of accountancy as a genuine profession. The consequences of the growth of both multinational business and multinational audit firms, with arguably less-perfect competition among the latter, are areas of 'process' and 'context' in which academic accountants should increase their research and strengthen their intellectual contribution.

Public Sector Accounting

One subject area where accounting research has increased substantially in recent years is the public sector. This may seem paradoxical in that, in the UK and many other countries, the public sector appears to be contracting, at the same time as research expands. But firstly, the contraction of the public sector may in one sense be illusory. The proportion of gross domestic product given over to public spending in the UK has not declined much, but what has happened is that the proportion of public spending on transfer payments (for welfare, pensions, EU contributions etc.), and the proportion of public spending committed through a mixture of executive agencies, quangos, private firms and voluntary bodies held at arm's length from government, have increased rapidly at the expense of spending on services dispensed directly by government employees and departments. That is, the national government has become an enabler and financier of public services, more than a direct provider. The National Health Service supplies a good example of this, with its purchaser-provider split: commissioning health authorities are centrally funded and accountable under central government resource accounting; while the hospital and other service providers, organised as quasi-autonomous Trusts, will account and be audited independently (although within government guidelines).

A second likely reason for expansion of public sector research is the interest created by the scale of change and modernisation of public sector accounting and budgeting methods in the UK. An early example arose when water (and sewage) was removed from local government in 1974 and reorganised as regional water authorities: traditional local government accounting was replaced by full accrual accounting, by 'best commercial practice' except that replacement values were adopted for asset valuation and devaluation. This variation on CCA risked overstatement of depreciation, and of charges, and these are issues to which we return again later. The NHS also gradually improved its accounting, costing and budgeting, finally moving to full accrual accounting after 1990 with the internal market reorganisations: but all this was a slow process, very expensive in terms of new computer systems, consultants and expanded accounting staffing, and the NHS has been open to public censure when apparently expanding accounting and managerial jobs at a time when the numbers of nurses were falling. The total cost of upgrading NHS non-clinical IT, management and accounting is unknown, but over the last five years this may well have greatly exceeded £2bn: it is a great act of faith that this enormous investment at the opportunity cost of forgone spending on direct health care has been worthwhile, and definitive research on this is needed and awaited.

Perhaps the most dramatic upgrading of public sector accounting has been in central government itself, with the publication of a White Paper (1995) on 'Resource Accounting and Budgeting in Government', behind which one imagines a strong academic input from Andrew Likierman. The key challenge here, it appears to me, is the balancing act between Parliamentary needs to determine and control funding on an annual cash basis, and operational management needs to manage and control budgets on an accrual basis, the better to assess resource consumption and managerial performance, especially as regards use of capital. It appears that each government department will be treated as a 'holding company', consolidating its own non-trading executive agencies and some other activities (such as NHS authorities). But it appears also that single consolidated accounts for central government as a whole will not be prepared - but that is an innovation which can and should come later.

Even New Zealand, which some observers consider to be the most advanced nation in applying business-style (accrual) accounting to the public sector, has not yet decided to proceed to full consolidation. Without full consolidation, it is not clear how parliamentarians and citizens can gain a good overview of the financial integrity and direction of public money. Without such consolidation and full reporting, the new UK resource accounting and budgeting reforms might be seen primarily as an exercise in management accounting only - that is, not a means of significantly improving public accountability, but rather mainly just a means of assisting Ministers, Cabinet and perhaps Parliament, to monitor performance and value-for-money against central policy objectives. I have a personal feeling that the New Zealand approach sets a higher value on public accountability. New Zealand differs from the UK also in applying the same Accounting Standards in the public sector as in the private sector, whereas the UK government will set its own standards in consultation with the Treasury's new Financial Reporting Advisory Board, whose future influence is moot.

Until recently, UK local government accounting was, although rigorous in its own way, following a system developed in Victorian times and enshrined and protected from change by out-of-date legislation. But local government accounting is now more in the mainstream - the main catalyst to provoke this to happen was the introduction of CCT (compulsory competitive tendering), whereby an increasing number of non-core and support services had to be opened to competition from private suppliers (as well as in-house teams). For this to work fairly it clearly was essential to have tenders and accounts on a comparable basis with the private sector, including proper depreciation charges and target returns on capital (albeit that the target returns were initially set in 'real terms', as a return on the replacement value of assets, whereas private firms were of course perfectly free to set tender prices as 'penetration prices' at levels well below long-term real costs).

Returning to New Zealand, it too has reformed local government accounting, again applying the same accounting standards as used for the private sector. There is no suggestion in New Zealand of consolidating local government accounts with central government: this is because they see the two levels of government as fully independent. In New Zealand, local government has a more limited range of services than in the UK, receives little funding from central government except for roads, and is more truly independent. There may be a moral here for the UK. It is not an accounting issue, but rather a political, financial and accountability issue. Local government would be healthier if central government took direct responsibility (possibly through new forms of executive agencies) for all public services which it directly funds and which are intended to provide more or less equal volumes and standards of service in all parts of the nation.

Local government, like other levels of government, could benefit from increased research. Social and environmental accounting research is clearly relevant throughout the public sector, and often it is easier to conduct in the public sector. One reason why I eventually settled into public sector research, was because I found it easier to get (probably) truthful research data 'on the record', warts and all, whereas my previous research in the private sector had often been frustrated by commercial confidentiality. And I was a gentleman researcher, not an investigative journalist. But I am afraid research is growing more difficult in the public sector - the introduction of a more competitive structure and business culture is making it more difficult for researchers to learn the truth.

Performance measurement, and the use of performance indicators in management, planning and resource allocation/contracting is another area needing greater public sector research. This arises because (most) public sector bodies are not profit seeking, nor profit-maximising. They have no quantifiable single objective, like profit. They are, broadly, service maximisers - but usually they provide a number, and sometimes a great number, of divisibly separate services. And ideally the services should be judged for quality and relevance, not just volume and unit-cost minimisation. Or, in a complex service such as the NHS, they should be judged on the 'outcomes', not just the 'outputs', and certainly not just the 'economy of inputs' measures which provided nearly all the performance measurements available until a few years ago. Both the NHS and local government, under central government pressure, have developed literally hundreds of performance indicators, but the bulk of these do not go beyond efficiency and outputs, so much research remains to develop better measures, for effectiveness and outcomes.

An area of research deserving greater attention for the public sector is transfer pricing theory. I recently examined a PhD thesis on costing and pricing for contracts in the NHS internal market. The thesis did not mention transfer pricing as a basis, or even as a benchmark, for setting NHS prices. I was annoyed with the student, at least until I established that transfer pricing had been discussed, but the internal research supervisor had advised it was not relevant nor needful to be considered in the thesis. In effect, the academic supervisor had taken at face value the governments' pronouncements that contracting should be fully at arm's length in the NHS, ignoring all interdependencies and opportunities for economy through sharing, specialisation and other forms of cooperation as distinct from competition. I personally hold that two-part tariff transfer pricing (David Solomons, 1965) successfully combines both economic principles and practical awareness of management behaviour and incentives, and that it should be tested out widely in public sector research and modelling.

Reform of public sector accounting may not be sufficient without parallel reform of public sector accountability. The government has sensibly required my local authorities to send me, with my Council Tax demands, brief but informative financial and performance reports. But the UK government does not send me a similar report, consolidated or otherwise, of its own financial and service performance. I think it should do so. Of course, various researchers have concluded that voters do not pay great attention to governmental financial reports (although there may be greater interest in budgets, when published). But it is also claimed that company shareholders do not pay great attention to annual financial reports, nor usually react to them strongly for pricing judgements and buy/sell decisions. Yet it is seldom suggested that company annual accounts and reports do not provide a useful backstop for credibility and probity, or that they should not be made public to stakeholders. I await receiving an annual financial report from my government, and I shall wish to take a particular interest in their capital accounting and their accountability for capital maintenance.

Public Capital

As a stakeholder in Great Britain plc, I should be very interested to know what is the value of my stake in the public capital. Current public sector accounting in Britain (as in most other countries) denies me this information. Is my stake £10,000 or £15,000 or what? Is it rising or falling? Is the capital value being maintained - in real terms? And if it is not being maintained, why so, and how and where are the equivalent cash flows being diverted, or the capital and other debt adjustments being made?

This section of the essay has but little to say regarding accounting 'process' - partly because there has been no coherent process for developing public sector accounting principles, or practices. Each of the major public services (e.g. Water, before privatisation, and the NHS), individual nationalised industries (before privatisation), central government, and local government, all have had their accounting systems developed originally from separate historical roots and then reformed to their present states by separate initiatives, at different times, and without much if any commonality of accounting principles or concepts - although perhaps one linking feature in recent years has been adaptation to 'inflation accounting' following the Byatt Report (HM Treasury, 1986).

This section will briefly cite some of the features and problems of public sector capital accounting 'content', and will mention some problems of capital accounting 'context' because only from awareness of public sector accounting, capable of meaningful consolidation into genuinely integrated national accounts.

Harold Macmillan observed that in times of difficulty, families would "sell some of their assets: first the Georgian silver goes". He was referring to the tendency of government in recent years to sell off nationalised industries, and also public buildings and land including playing fields, to realise their capital value. Under the entity theory of accounting, such capital receipts can be used legitimately either to purchase other capital assets, or to reduce capital debt. Unfortunately, British central government accounting does not effectively distinguish between capital debt and revenue debt, in the PSBR (the Public Sector Borrowing Requirement). Thus government accounting fails to give evidence that capital receipts have not been diverted to finance cuts in income tax - the rough equivalence of which in the private sector would be using capital proceeds to finance increased dividends on a contracting capital investment base, a practice which ought to demand and receive the fullest accounting disclosure, and accountability.

My own research involvement with public sector capital accounting arose several years before the 'family silver' problem materialised. During the early 1970s it appeared that the then government was possibly exerting some pressure on nationalised industries to understate (at a time of fairly high inflation) their real depreciation costs. The motive for this was suspected to be the desire to hold down nationalised industry prices because of the latter's effect on the RPI and thus on further inflationary wage claims. A grant was raised to research this problem, by attempting to compare and evaluate public sector capital accounting across a range of major public sector organisations. Irvine Lapsley was the lead researcher on this project. Good cooperation was obtained from the NHS, local authorities and water authorities, but for reasons perhaps obvious if regrettable, the information obtainable from nationalised industries was not as detailed or profound as was sought.

At that time, in the mid-1970s, NHS accounting was on an income and expenditure basis with limited accruals for debtors and creditors, but with no accrual accounting for capital and depreciation. These accruals for debtors and creditors, but with no accrual accounting for capital and depreciation. These accounts were reconciled annually against the cash allocations received by each health authority. The cash accounts provided the true control. Cash used for capital spending was effectively expensed, or 100% depreciated, in the year of spending. Challenging this at the Ministry elucidated the response that since Parliament was supreme and could alter its plans and desires from year to year, it would not be acceptable to spread the cost of capital consumption over the useful life of assets, as distinct from the year of actual expenditure.

By the mid-1970s individuals in local authorities had already been worrying about their method of accounting for capital assets and consumption for over half a century, but nothing had been done. Capital assets could be acquired by funding from capital borrowing, by votes from revenue funding, by purchase from a repairs and renewals fund, or by donations. Each source of funding received a different accounting treatment, at the extremes involving either 100% expensing in the year of acquisition, or, retaining 100% of original cost on the books until final disposal of the assets. I recall Professor Will Baxter, at one seminar on these practices, expressing his total dismay!

Local government's major source for funding capital assets was from borrowed capital. This was accounted-for by 'loan charge accounting', involving charging service accounts the annual portion of capital borrowing repaid, plus interest on remaining capital borrowing. Although not formally depreciation accounting, the resulting total charges were similar to annuity depreciation on historical cost - a method highly defensible in a low-risk environment, provided the capital borrowing period was largely the same as the period of useful asset life. But also, frequently these periods were not the same, sometimes because of central government diktats on allowable borrowing periods, and there was always the problem of inflation affecting long-life assets.

Water authorities were the third of the areas for which good research evidence was established, and which were compared in Perrin (1981). Following the 1974 reorganisation, water authorities had to abandon local government accounting and move swiftly to full accrual accounting, including asset underground pipes, water and sewage treatment plants), accountants were at the mercy of managers and technical experts in assessing condition, useful life, and replacement costs. Since water-charging was a cost-plus monopoly, the suspicion lingers that the benefit of the doubt was given to understating asset lives, and perhaps overstating replacement valuations, so as to justify higher-than-true depreciation charges, and thus higher water charges. Of course, with privatisation these uncertainties are now just water under the bridge - or are they? Good accounting for regulated utilities may have much in common with good accounting for fee-charging public services. For the nationalised water authorities there was a suspicion that high depreciation and charges were facilitating the internal (but hidden) self-financing of capital assets, reducing debate to justify investment. For privatised water corporations there may still be suspicion, that excessive depreciation charges in regulated prices may somehow metamorphose by creative accounting into unearned dividends or diversified investments irrelevant to the public services for which regulated monopoly was granted.

During the 1970s an extended series of seminars on the water industry were held at York university by Alan Williams. Ian Byatt and Bryan Carsberg, and I and others, all participated in examining related issues on investment, pricing, accounting and depreciation, for Water. Privatisation was not foreseen. Economic concepts dominated. There was no agreement on whether or not all water users should have water meters: however, there is now some evidence that during last summer's drought many flat-charge water users failed to restrain their consumption, possibly because privatised water is no longer seen as a public good with any obligation of conscience to share and conserve, but rather now as just another commodity from which to take as much as you can, for whatever you are forced to pay.

Universal water metering may now become essential in order to conserve water, and it is only with universal metering that accountants can determine, and the regulator and consumer validate, that pricing is fair relative to costs. At the York seminars the traditional view dominated that utility pricing was fair on the basis of a standing charge to cover fixed costs of service provision, plus a unit-variable charge for the volume of consumer use. Fair or not in economic terms, this pricing system places a greater unit-cost burden on smaller volume users. This is not a system which is fair in social equity terms, nor unit-cost burden on smaller volume users. This is not a system which is fair in social equity terms, nor does it encourage reduced consumption of a scarce resource, in this case water. Social equity and environment logic would suggest abolishing standing charges, a low price for small consumption of (metered) water, and a scale of rising prices for larger quantities: accountants could research on long-term cost relationships for such pricing, but since in the short term this pricing structure would be the opposite to the signals from short-term marginal costs, its use in the real world could come about only if required by Parliament and enforced by regulators.

Capital Maintenance & Inter-generational Equity

There can be little dispute of the claim that British sewers and water distribution networks deteriorated for at least sixty years before the 1974 water industry reorganisation: the British people relied on the capital investment of Victorian and Edwardian times, and we did not reinvest adequately. Lack of proper depreciation accounting, and of proper accounting disclosure, reporting and publicity may provide some explanation, or even excuse. Since 1974 the pendulum may have swung the other way, with current systems and levels of charges providing finance for improvements greater than currently needed (provided the finance is ring-fenced so as not to leak to diversified investment outside Water).

Thus, neither before nor after 1974 was investment at a level which could be measured and debated as fair and reasonable in the context of maintaining capital stock (and value) from one generation to another, for equity in charges and in quality of service delivery.

Maintaining inter-generational equity in the stock of public capital is not a social, ethical or managerial principle to which UK governments have paid noticeable attention. A good excuse for this is that accountants have not provided and published or publicised good quality information on the cost and value of capital stock, on the spending on maintenance compared to the rate of decay/consumption, and on the net increase or decrease from year to year in capital stock (and thus the net change in inter-generational equity). I believe that accountants should be required to work out fair and true measures for reporting all this, and that governments should be required to publish full information on public capital (maintenance) and to be held fully accountable before people and parliament.

Obviously recent governments have downsized the public sector by privatisation. In one sense this has been publicly accounted for, as a policy issue, but no full accounting has been made as to the amount of the (possibly unnecessary) loss of book value and economic value of assets through discount selling in flotations. There have also been massive transaction costs borne by the public, not prominently accounted for. And currently there is the major unfinished privatisation of the railways, with a background of alleged massive under-investment or deferred investment during the preparational stages.

Water aside, most of the privatisations have been of publicly owned activities either not inherently public services, or not inherently needing to be provided as monopolies (and therefore at extra risk of abuse if not directly provided for the public by government). However, the more traditional public services are also at risk of capital run-down, or of postponement of capital maintenance so that future generations will be left to pay for backlog-maintenance as well as fur current maintenance. Currently there are large capital spending reductions on road building and public housing, on the NHS (where a cut of £600mn over two years has been mentioned in a private Executive briefing), in higher education (where vice-chancellors threatened to impose a university entry fee to claw back a 33% cut in capital funding), and in schools. For schools, the Minister recently called upon local authorities to sell any surplus school land and buildings and use the proceeds for repairs to the remaining schools: this of course would involve realising capital funds to divert them to revenue account spending, possibly useful but involving a reduction in the stock of public sector capital probably without full accounting disclosure or debate of public (inter-generational equity) accountability.

It has been suggested that the present government may have a number of reasons and motives for the current cuts in public sector capital spending. It is said that they do not actually like the public sector, and will not be unhappy to see it appear grotty and decayed, providing this does not lose votes. It is argued that they need to cut public spending to create headroom for tax cuts, and/or to reduce the PSBR to strengthen their bargaining position in the European Union. It is also possible that they see the PFI (Private Finance Initiative) as an effective means of disassembling the public sector (by removing effective control of public assets from elected bodies and public servants). But the actual flow of capital cash from the PFI has so far been slow, and an inter-generational backlog is accumulating. Moreover, capital funds provided through PFI involve higher 'interest' costs than traditional public borrowing, as well as high transaction costs, so that under PFI and annualised capital use/consumption costs of public sector capital (and thus the long-term taxation costs) are bound to rise - unless the costs and disciplines of PFI inherently lead the public sector to be substantially more cost-efficient in using capital, although that is a hypothesis testable only over an extended period of years.

The government is politically entitled to scale down the public sector, and to allow the deterioration of public assets by restricting revenue funding for maintenance, and capital funding for replacement - provided, that is, it has an electoral mandate for this. But it can only have a legitimated electoral mandate if the public are informed as to the policy, its costs and benefits, and its long-term as well as short-term implications. At present these conditions clearly are not met. And one main reason for this is the absence of adequate accounting (and economic) measurements, analysis, reporting and public attention. There thus exists enormous scope for the improved development of public sector accounting (process and content), or if government does not will this to happen, then a useful if second-best solution is for academics to conduct context research not just for intellectual interest, but in hope of informing public understanding and assisting rational political judgement.

Conclusion

After a wider opening, this paper focused on the specialised issue of problems in public sector capital management, and of the inadequacy of current accounting and reporting systems to place all the facts before people and Parliament, to improve accountability and to assist governmental policy and practice to meet the public will. And probably this cannot be achieved without full consolidation of all central government accounts and finances, and concise reporting annually with tax returns and through the press. The state of public capital maintenance and inter-generational equity should be made crystal clear. Meanwhile, academic accountants may conclude that little if anything has yet been discovered as eternal truths for accounting. Accounting needs change with a changing world. "Though the way be weary", accounting research must continue, deepen, expand, and "Keep right on to the end".

References

Accounting Standards Board (1995) <u>Statement of Principles for Financial Reporting</u>, Exposure Draft.

Accounting Standards Steering Committee (1975) <u>The Corporate Report</u>, a discussion paper.

Angell, I. (1995) 'Winners and Losers in the Information Age', <u>LSE Magazine</u>, Centenary Issue, Summer.

Baxter, W.T. (1971) <u>Depreciation</u>, Sweet & Maxwell.

Baxter, W.T. (1975) <u>Accounting Values and Inflation</u>, McGraw-Hill.

Baxter, W.T. (1978) <u>Collected Papers on Accounting</u>, Arno Press.

Baxter, W.T. (1984) <u>Inflation Accounting</u>, Philip Allan.

Baxter, W.T. & S. Davidson (1962) <u>Studies in Accounting Theory</u>, Sweet & Maxwell.

<u>Better Accounting for the Taxpayer's Money</u> (1995) The Government's Proposals, Resource Accounting and Budgeting in Government, Cm2929, HMSO.

Bromwich, M. & A.G. Hopwood (1981) (eds) <u>Essays in British Accounting Research</u>, Pitman.

Forker, J. (1996) Review of Zeff & Dharan (q.v.) <u>Readings and Notes on Financial Accounting</u>, in <u>The British Accounting Review</u>, Vol.28, No.1, March.

HM Treasury (1986) <u>Accounting for Economic Costs and Changing Prices</u> (the Byatt Report), HMSO.

Lawson, G.H. (1981) 'The Cash Flow Performance of UK Companies: case studies in cash flow accounting', in Bromwich & Hopwood (q.v.).

Lee, T.A. (1981) 'Cash Flow Accounting and Corporate Financial Reporting', in Bromwich & Hopwood (q.v.).

Lee, T.A. (1995) 'The Professionalization of Accountancy: a history of protecting the public interest in a self-interested way', in <u>Accounting Auditing & Accountability Journal</u>, Vol.8, No.4.

Perrin, J. (1981) 'Accounting Research in the Public Sector', in Bromwich & Hopwood (q.v.).

Solomons, D. (1965) <u>Divisional Performance: measurement and control</u>, Irwin.

<u>UK GAAP</u> (1994) Generally accepted accounting practice in the United Kingdom, Ernst & Young and Macmillan.

Whittington, G. (1995) 'Is Accounting Becoming too Interesting?', the Sir Julian Hodge Lecture, University College of Wales, Aberystwyth.

Whittington, G.(1996) 'Some Interesting Aspects of Accounting', Plenary address at the British Accounting Association 1996 National Conference, Cardiff.

Zeff, S.A. and B.G. Dharan (1994) <u>Readings and Notes on Financial Accounting: Issues and Controversies</u>, 4th edn., McGraw-Hill.

INCOME MEASUREMENT, REPORTING ENTITIES AND SHARE-BASED COMPENSATION

John Forker

Introduction

The exercise of choice among different accounting concepts and practices is inevitable when preparing financial statements. Opinions differ, however, about the freedom of choice which ought to be available to preparers of financial statements. For some, a framework for the regulation of accounting practice is essential (Stamp, 1980, Solomons 1983[1]). If market discipline is inadequate the opportunistic have scope to engineer uncompensated wealth transfers by means of accounting policy choice. This undermines accountability. In this view to safeguard the credibility of financial statements, the task of selecting among concepts and rules ought to be delegated to a regulatory authority. Compliance with mandated requirements promotes comparability and accountability.

Those who place greater faith in the capacity of market competition to force the adoption of best accounting practice are more sceptical about the benefits from regulation. The main proponent of this school of thought is Baxter. For over forty years he has consistently and skilfully advocated the view that regulation stifles the development of accounting theory and best practice. In Baxter's opinion the threat is greatest when regulators choose among different accounting concepts (Baxter, 1953). Persistent public concern about the reliability of financial statements and consequent demand for tighter regulation favours those in the debate who advocate more regulation and less choice for preparers of financial statements.

The issue of the extent of regulation is, however, secondary. More important, as a basis for choice, is the need for a clear understanding of the nature of different accounting concepts. It is in this area that Baxter's contribution has been pre-eminent. Accounting is a relatively young academic discipline where justification is difficult. In particular, vested interests have much to protect and many of the parties to the debate have not had the advantage of a rigorous academic training in the subject. Not surprisingly, there is much scope, and incentive, for muddled thought and inconsistency. As a writer and educator Baxter has been tireless in the clear and lucid exposition of accounting theory and merciless in exposing unsound dogma.

In the spirit of Baxter's work this essay explores the differences between two models of the reporting entity. One serves as the basis for measuring income in the US and the other is the preferred choice in the UK. The models are variants of the general Assets less Liabilities equals Equity model (A-L=E). They differ with respect to the classification of financial instruments as either equity or as liabilities. In these models issuing financial instruments to acquire resources, on terms that dilute the interest of the pre-existing shareholders, gives rise to different measures of income.

The US preferred model treats all equity as homogeneous for the purpose of income measurement: in this essay it is referred to as the equity model (EM). The model proposed for the UK is more narrowly focused on the interest of the pre-existing equity shareholders and will be referred to as the pre-existing equity model (PEEM). In the US the choice of the EM has been the subject of careful consideration of the differences between the two models (FASB, 1990). The same cannot be said for the UK. The ASB has not promoted discussion of the differences between the models. Also, the draft (ASB, Chapter 3, 1992) and subsequent exposure draft of the Statement of Principles (ASB, 1995) do not provide unambiguous definitions of equity and liabilities for the selected model of the reporting entity.

Accounting for share based compensation clearly reveals the differential impact of model choice on income measurement. It is also the subject of a highly controversial standard in the US (FAS123, FASB,1995). This was mainly due to the unfavourable impact of the proposals on income. This essay extends beyond explaining differences between the models. It also presents a neat and powerful solution for resolving the differences between the models when accounting for share-based compensation. The solution, which has wider applications, is based on Lindahl's (1939) dictum that windfalls ought to be excluded from income and accounted for as a capital adjustment. For exercised share options the proposed accounting treatment for windfalls thus gives rise to a lower charge against income. In the

A-L=E model, the solution requires a refinement of the conventional definitions applied to liabilities and non-reciprocal transfers arising from transactions with owners.

Consideration of the work of Lindahl has wider implications for the academic training of accountants. Insights from economics have inspired much of Baxter's accounting thought. The ever increasing burden of compliance with check lists of regulatory pronouncements has reduced the time available to study the contribution of economists to the theory of income measurement. This is a pity. On the limited evidence of this essay the task of selecting accounting concepts would benefit from the application of economic insights into the measurement of income. Further, in support of Baxter's thesis, adoption of a specific model for measuring income by the FASB appears to have stifled creative thought and, in the case of share-based compensation, has given rise to wooden handed regulation.

The comparative analysis of the PEEM and the EM in this essay does not provide a basis for ranking the respective models. Choice among different models for measuring income ought to be based on a wide ranging consideration of many factors extending beyond those in the shareholder orientated PEEM and EM. Such an analysis is beyond the scope of this essay. For this reason the first section of the essay places these models in a wider context. There then follows a description of the boundaries for the classification of equity and liability financing instruments in the respective models. Various measurement issues and the effect of model choice on income measurement serve to complicate expense recognition and require careful consideration. However, application of Lindahl's dictum that windfalls from share-based compensation be excluded from income resolves the differences in measuring income between the two models. Finally, after a brief review of the US and UK proposals for share-based compensation, the recommendations follow.

Income concepts and boundaries of the reporting entity

A useful conceptual starting point is provided by Fisher's (1906) concept of income as consumption. As illustrated in Figure 1, from this flows the different measures proposed by Schmidt (1921), Lindahl (1939) and Hicks (1939). Schmidt is primarily concerned with measuring income for business enterprises. Lindahl and Hicks adopt a more general approach and focus on how to deal with problems associated with the resolution of uncertainty and differences in interest rates. As illustrated in Figure 1, the models considered in this essay fall within the sub-set maintaining the financial value of capital. Specifically, in the PEEM and EM different concepts of ownership wealth serve as the basis for measuring capital. These models reflect the predominant focus on reporting to shareholders in the legal and accounting contexts of the UK and US.

In terms of Figure 1, the FASB and the ASB have chosen financial capital maintenance of the residual equity interest given by A-L=E. Income is measured by the change in the equity residual, after excluding transactions with owners relating to contributions and distributions of capital. All recognised gains and losses are included in income; hence the measure is generally known as comprehensive income. For example, in FRS3 (ASB,1992) comprehensive income is the sum of profit (loss) plus other recognised gains (losses) reported in the Statement of Recognised Holding Gains and Losses (SRHGL).

The two main versions of the A-L=E model reflect different views of the extent of the equity residual. In the first alternative, the reporting entity is restricted to the interests of the pre-existing equity. An important feature of the pre-existing equity model (PEEM) is that no distinction is made between the enterprise as an economic unit and the interest of the pre-existing equity shareholders. In the PEEM, ownership rights are viewed as if they are assets of the entity. Thus, an undertaking to issue equity to a third party is viewed, not as an non-reciprocal transfer[2] but as an exchange transaction which commits the entity to deliver resources. In the PEEM these commitments are classified as liabilities: the prudence convention applies and changes in the value of the liability is reflected in income. Specifically, an obligation to issue equity for less than market value is classified as a liability and any cost of dilution is charged against income.

The second version of the A-L=E views the reporting entity as an economic unit distinct and separate from the equity interest. In terms of the general A-L=E model, and in contrast to the PEEM, the equity residual is expanded to encompass all equity funding instruments including derivative securities. Consequently, the definition of liabilities is restricted to obligations to commit resources of the economic unit, and these exclude ownership rights. Transactions in ownership rights, broadly defined, are classified as non-reciprocal transfers and do not effect income. To reflect the adoption of a wider view of the ownership residual this version of A-L=E is described as the equity model (EM).

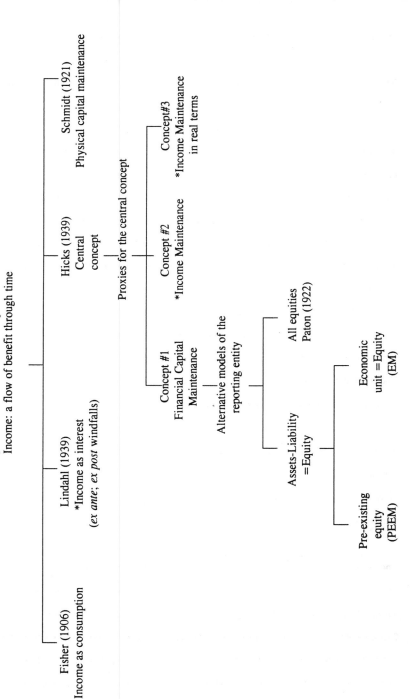

Theory of Income Measurement

Fisher (1906)
Capital: a stock of benefits at a point in time
Income: a flow of benefit through time

Fisher (1906)
Income as consumption

Lindahl (1939)
*Income as interest
(ex ante; ex post windfalls)

Hicks (1939)
Central
concept

Schmidt (1921)
Physical capital maintenance

Proxies for the central concept

Concept #1
Financial Capital
Maintenance

Concept #2
*Income Maintenance

Concept#3
*Income Maintenance
in real terms

Alternative models of the
reporting entity

All equities
Paton (1922)

Assets-Liability
=Equity

Economic
unit =Equity
(EM)

Pre-existing
equity
(PEEM)

* Under uncertainty : windfall (unexpected) changes in value excluded from *ex post* income.

Measurement of share-based compensation expense depends on the valuation methods applied to options and on the model of the reporting entity used to measure income. Issues relating to valuation are set out in Figure 2 and Table 1. For valuation purposes there are three main dates in the life of an option. These are described as measurement dates because the share price[3] (S) on the respective dates serves as the basis for measuring the value of an option (c). The first of these is the date when the option is granted (S_o,c_o). Next, the vesting date occurs when the option holder has complied with the conditions of service (S_v,c_v). These relate to the completion of a specified period of employment after the grant of the option and, increasingly, include specific performance hurdles. The period from the date of grant to the date of vesting is also known as the service period and, generally, is the period over which compensation cost is accrued. The final date is the date of exercise (S_t,c_T).

Figure 2: Valuation Criteria for Share-Based Compensation

DATES

GRANT	VESTING	EXERCISE

SERVICE PERIOD

| S_o | S_v | S_T |
| (c_o) | (c_v) | (c_T) |

SHARE PRICE

(AND OPTION VALUE)

LEGEND:

S_o, S_v and S_T:	are, respectively, share prices at dates of grant, vesting and exercise
c_o, c_v and c_T:	are, respectively, option values at dates of grant, vesting and exercise
GRANT DATE:	date on which contract is entered into; is conditional on delivery of service and payment of exercise price.
VESTING DATE:	date when service conditions are complied with; regarded by some as the issue date.
EXERCISE DATE:	option holder pays exercise price (X) and company settles the obligation.
SERVICE PERIOD:	the period during which the employee performs the service in exchange for the award of share options.

Table 1: ACCOUNTING FOR SHARE-BASED COMPENSATION
VALUATION ALTERNATIVES

MEASUREMENT DATES	MEASUREMENT METHODS		
	INTRINSIC VALUE	MINIMUM VALUE	FAIR VALUE
GRANT DATE (c_o)	$S_0 - X$	$S_0 - Xe^{-rft}$	$S_0 N(d_1) - Xe^{-rft} N(d_2)$
VESTING DATE (c_v)	$S_V - X$	$S_V - Xe^{-rft}$	$S_V N(d_1) - Xe^{-rft}$
EXERCISE DATE (c_t)	$S_T - X$	$S_T - X$	$S_T - X$

LEGEND:

S_0, S_V, S_T and X: see Figure 2

FAIR VALUE: is the Black and Scholes (1973) option pricing formula where

r_f: is the risk free rate of interest
t: is the time to maturity of the option
N(d):is the cumulative normal density function and,

$$d_1 = \frac{\ln(S/X) + r_f t}{\sigma\sqrt{t}} + \frac{1}{2}\sigma\sqrt{t}$$

$$d_2 = d_1 - \sigma\sqrt{t}$$

where σ is the standard deviation of the continuously compounded annual rate of return on the share

There are a variety of measurement methods which can be applied to the share price on the respective measurement dates. The three main alternatives are considered in this essay. The application of three measurement methods to a share price on three measurement dates provides nine different values. These are set out in Table 1[4]. The first measurement method is known as the intrinsic value method and has the merit of simplicity. The cost of the option to the company is given by the difference between the share price, at each of the measurement dates, and the exercise price. Intrinsic value has two obvious attractions. It avoids computational difficulties and, secondly, for the grant date alternative it provides a measure of compensation cost of zero for most options. Not surprisingly intrinsic value is the conventionally applied method in the UK.

The second alternative is the minimum value method. The minimum amount a company granting an option can expect to receive is the difference between the current share price and the present value of the exercise price. The value attributable to options from the volatility of the share price is ignored but, as with the intrinsic value approach, there are no computational difficulties.

The final method calculates the fair value of the option. All factors impacting on the cost of the option to the issuer are relevant. Specifically, option pricing models are applied to incorporate the effect of share price volatility. Also, the impact on the cost of options of anticipated dividends, non-transferability and the prospect of forfeiture must be taken into account. For grant date and vesting date measurement the fair value method is particularly subjective. However, in the case of exercise date measurement, there is no subjectivity. The cost of options on the date of exercise is uniform across measurement methods and is given by the difference between the share price on the date of exercise and the exercise price, S_T-X.

Measurement of compensation expense: models of the reporting entity

An added dimension of the measurement issue, not reflected in Table 1, is the effect different models of the reporting entity have on expense recognition. Table 2 sets out the factors which give rise to differences between the PEEM and EM. The fundamental factor determining the accounting treatment for option schemes is whether they are classified as liability or equity financing instruments. The

112

boundary of the reporting entity provides the basis for the classification.

<u>Table 2: MEASUREMENT OF COMPENSATION EXPENSE</u>
<u>MODELS, CLASSIFICATION OF SCHEMES AND CHARGE FOR DILUTION</u>
<u>IN THE PROFIT AND LOSS ACCOUNT</u>

Reporting entities	Equity	Liabilities
	Cost of dilution at date of grant or date of vesting charged in P&L	Full cost of dilution at date of exercise charged in P & L
Pre-existing (PEEM)	N/A	All option schemes
Equity model (EM)	Shares issued	Cash Based Settlement

In the PEEM, the boundary of the reporting entity is restricted to the interest of the pre-existing equity shareholders. Changes in the value of the entity are reflected in income with the exception of those classified as non-reciprocal transfers. The latter are one-sided and do not oblige the recipient to deliver resources in exchange. In the context of the PEEM, non-reciprocal transfers are restricted to pre-existing equity contributions and distributions of capital. No distinction exists between the entity and its owners, thus the assets of the entity include ownership rights. Commitments to issue equity to a third party are viewed as exchange transactions and are classified as liabilities.

The implication for measuring share based compensation is that all option schemes are treated uniformly irrespective of whether the option is settled by the issue of new shares or by cash based methods of settlement. Hence, the convention of prudence when accounting for liabilities applies. In terms of Table 1 the appropriate measurement date is the exercise date. Changes in the value of options prior to expiry, or exercise, are recognised and included in income. The result is that for exercised options the full cost of dilution, S_T-X, is charged against income.

In the EM, measurement of compensation expense is complicated by differences in the methods of servicing exercised options. The method of settlement determines the classification of options as either equity or liabilities. Thus, for otherwise identical option schemes the charge against income is different.

By virtue of the separation between the economic unit and ownership, interest transactions in ownership, rights fall outside the boundary of the EM. Option schemes which commit the entity to issue new shares are classified as equity. In the EM, when shares are issued they are valued at the consideration received i.e. the exercise price. Although this practice is inconsistent with the principle of fair value accounting, it does reflect the impact of the transaction on the boundary of the EM. Thus, costs of dilution suffered by pre-existing equity when options are exercised are not recognised for equity funded option schemes. Costs of dilution arising from transactions between pre-existing equity and a third party do not impact on income: they are merely wealth transfers within equity.

TABLE 3: SHARE-BASED COMPENSATION
COMPARATIVE CHARACTERISTICS OF ALTERNATIVE
MODELS OF THE REPORTING ENTITY

CHARACTERISTICS	PRE-EXISTING EQUITY MODEL (PEEM)	EQUITY MODEL (EM)
CHARGE FOR COMPENSATION EXPENSE INDEPENDENT OF METHOD OF FUNDING	✓	X
FULL COST OF DILUTION ACCOUNTED FOR AS LOSS TO PRE-EXISTING SHAREHOLDERS	✓	X
NEW ISSUES VALUED AT MARKET VALUE	✓	X
NEW ISSUES VALUED AT CONSIDERATION RECEIVED	X	✓

✓: MODEL COMPLIES WITH CHARACTERISTIC

X : MODEL DOES NOT COMPLY WITH CHARACTERISTIC

In contrast, methods of settlement committing the entity to cash payments on exercise, either by purchasing existing shares, or a cash payment equal to S_T-X, are classified as liabilities. In this case a commitment exists to deliver resources of the entity; this is an exchange transaction. The recognition and measurement of compensation expense is the same as for the PEEM and the full cost of dilution is charged against income. The differences when accounting for share-based compensation in the PEEM and the EM are summarised in Table 3.

Choice of measurement date in the equity model

In the EM, the choice of measurement date for equity instruments is restricted to the date of grant or the date of vesting[6]. Advocates of the former consider the cost to the entity to be set on the earliest date for the performance of the services; in effect at the start of the contract. Vesting date measurement is favoured by those who take the view that measurement should occur only on the date the security is issued. Supporters of vesting date measurement consider to this to be the date when the service obligations under the contract have been fulfilled.

Depending on whether grant or vesting date measurement is adopted, the costs of dilution for equity instruments will be restricted to the charge for compensation cost recognised on the respective measurement dates. If, however, the method of settlement involves a commitment to deliver resources of the entity i.e. a cash payment reducing its resources, the obligation is classified as a liability. The accounting rules for liabilities apply and the full cost of dilution is recognised.

It is important when considering measurement issues not to lose sight of the accounting context which, for the accruals process, requires *ex ante* an estimate of the cost of employee options. Thus, irrespective of the measurement date, it is necessary to estimate compensation expense in order to allocate cost over the service period. It has been observed that by delaying valuation until uncertainty has been resolved i.e. until the option is exercised or lapses, an advantage of the liability method is that it avoids difficult issues relating to non-transferability, forfeitability and estimation of volatility (AAA, (1994), FASB, 1995, para., 134). This is an invalid assertion if compensation is to be accrued over the service period. Arguably, use of a suitably adapted option pricing model provides the best estimate of the present value of the eventual liability.

Insights from the theory of income measurement

In the context of the theory of income measurement, Lindahl (1939) proposed separate definitions of income *ex ante* and income *ex post*. In a world of uncertainty the arrival of new information changes the expectations on which asset values are based. Consequently when measuring income, start of period and end of period asset values based on information at the beginning and end of an accounting period are not comparable. Income *ex ante* is based on start of period information applied to start and end of period asset values. In contrast, income *ex post* is based on end of period information applied to beginning and end of period values. The difference between the respective measures of income, attributable to changed expectations, is the windfall gain or loss.

A numerical illustration is provided in Table 4. The exclusion of a windfall loss of £8.33 from Lindahl's income *ex post* £18.33, is contrasted with the income of £10 arising under comprehensive income (Hicksian capital maintenance income concept number 1, in Figure 1) which includes the effect of the windfall. Lindahl, supported by Hicks (1939) and Kaldor (1955), advocated the exclusion of windfalls from the calculation of income *ex post*. In principle, income is a flow from a stock of capital (Fisher, 1906). Windfall effects do not flow from the stock of capital, rather they reflect changes in the stock of capital and ought to be excluded from the measurement of income. The merit of Lindahl's approach is that income *ex post* is unambiguously measured as a flow from a stock of capital, the value of which is revised in the light of end of period information. Under capital maintenance, differences in the information applied to asset values at the beginning and end of a period cause flows and stock (windfall) changes to be combined.

The notion of windfalls arising from the resolution of uncertainty applies directly to the measurement of share-based compensation[7]. In terms of Lindahl's analysis, date of grant measurement provides the value *ex ante* of an option at the beginning of the contract. A useful insight for accounting purposes is that subsequent changes in value attributable to new information are windfall effects. In accordance with the dictum that windfalls should be excluded from income *ex post* it follows that the cost at the date of grant is the appropriate basis for measuring compensation expense. If vesting or exercise date measurement is adopted changes in value after the date of grant ought, in principle, be excluded from income and accounted for as a windfall change in the stock of capital attributable to the reporting entity.

Definition of the elements of financial statements

Application of Lindahl's insight when accounting for share based compensation requires an amendment to the conventional definitions applied to financial statements. Under Hicksian capital maintenance, in particular A-L=E, changes in the valuation of liabilities impact on comprehensive income. Thus,

TABLE 4: COMPARISON OF COMPREHENSIVE INCOME AND LINDAHL'S *EX POST* INCOME AS INTEREST WITH WINDFALL VALUE CHANGES EXCLUDED

At time t_0 you expect to receive £110 at the end of the year (t_1) and expect the annual rate of interest to be 10%.

At t_1 you receive £110 as expected but the rate of interest throughout the period was not 10% but was 20%.

In general W_{jk} is wealth valued on basis of expectations held at time j applied to capital at time k.

	t_0		t_1
	—		—
Ex Ante (W_{oo})	100	.1	
			110(W_{11})
Ex Post Hindsight Value: (W_{10})	91.66	.2	

(1)   Comprehensive Income   £

   Ex Ante (W_{01}-W_{oo}) and *Ex Post* (W_{11}-W_{oo}) = 110-100   = <u>10</u>

(2)   Lindahl's Income as Interest

Ex Ante	$W_{oo}*r_0 = 100*(.1)$	= <u>10</u>
Ex Post	$W_{10}*r_1 = 91.66*(.2)$	= <u>18.33</u>
Windfall loss or Hindsight Capital Adjustment	$W_{10}-W_{oo} = 91.66-100$	= <u>(8.33)</u>

increases in the value of liabilities require a provision against income under application of the prudence convention. Following Lindahl, in the special case of share-based compensation, valuation changes after the date of grant have the character of windfalls. What is proposed is a refinement to the conventional definition of liabilities. In the A-L=E model, the definition of liabilities has to be revised to allow a departure from the rule that all increases in the value of liabilities be charged against income. Specifically, windfall changes in the value of liabilities would not require provisions against income. Rather, they would be accounted for as capital adjustments. In effect, windfalls are viewed as separate from the initial exchange transaction which gave rise to the liability. Consequently, within the A-L=E model, share option windfalls would be classified as non-reciprocal transfers. In general, these do not affect income, they are distinct from exchange transactions and are normally restricted to transactions with owners relating to contribution and distribution of capital. The proposed re-classification of windfalls on share options is consistent with the character of a non-reciprocal transfer: it changes the boundary of an entity, it is capital in nature and it is distinct from an exchange transaction which, in the case of share options, occurred at the date of grant.

The result, in the context of the A-L=E model, will be the elimination of income differences attributable to the classification of options schemes as either equity or liabilities. In both the PEEM and the EM the charge for compensation expense will be based on date of grant measurement. Irrespective of the classification of how option schemes are funded, subsequent valuation changes will be accounted for as capital adjustments. To ensure consistency between the models, and to allow full accountability for equity dilution, it will be necessary in the EM to recognise changes in the value of equity obligations as if they were liabilities. In effect, the principle of fair value accounting will apply equally to equity and liabilities. A simple numerical example illustrating the differences between the PEEM, the EM and the proposed approach is provided in Table 5. The example is based on a single year at the end of which the options either lapse or are exercised. The need to account for "unrealised" windfalls does not arise, but the accounting procedures would be identical.

Table 5

Accounting for share based compensation
Numerical illustration

Assume two options are granted at the start of an accounting period and, depending on the share price, are exercised or expire at the end of the period. They are otherwise identical except for the method of settlement. For one, the company is obliged to issue a new share; the other, a "stock appreciation right", is to be settled by cash payment equal to the difference between the share price and the exercise price.

The option details are:

	£
Share price at date of grant	400
Share price at date of: exercise	1000
or: expiry	300
Exercise price	400
Fair value of option when granted	100
Price paid by holder of an option	20

Accounting entries for three alternatives are illustrated; the pre-existing equity model (PEEM), the equity model (EM) and the approach advocated in this essay where windfalls are excluded from income. The result under either model is that the charge for compensation expense is based only on the date of grant cost. Irrespective of the model adopted there are no other income effects.

(A)   Accounting for compensation expense:

PEEM			EM			Windfalls excluded PEEM/EM		
Dr £	Cr £		Dr £	Cr £		Dr £	Cr £	
P&L 160			P&L 160			P&L 160		
Cash 40			Cash 40			Cash 40		
To Liability	200		To Liability	100		To Liability	100	
			Equity	100		Equity	100	

Share-based compensation based on date of grant fair value of the options.

(B)   Accounting for *ex post* windfall wealth transfers:

On exercise:

	PEEM Dr £	PEEM Cr £	EM Dr £	EM Cr £	Windfalls excluded PEEM/EM Dr £	Windfalls excluded PEEM/EM Cr £
P&L: Dilution	1000		500		-	
Liability	200		100		100	
Equity: Option					100	
Cash	800		800		800	
Equity: Dilution	-		-		1000	
To Equity		2000		1400		2000

PEEM	EM	Windfalls excluded PEEM/EM
Full cost of dilution on exercise charged against income	Share issued at consideration received, full cost of dilution charged in P&L on SAR	Share issued at fair value; full cost of dilution for both options accounted for as a capital loss

On Expiry:

	PEEM Dr £	PEEM Cr £		EM Dr £	EM Cr £		Windfalls excluded PEEM/EM Dr £	Windfalls excluded PEEM/EM Cr £
Liability	200		Liability	100		Liability	100	
						Equity: option	100	
To P&L		200	To P&L		100	To Equity		200

PEEM	EM	Windfalls excluded PEEM/EM
Gain on both options credited to income	Gain on SAR credited to income	Windfall gain on both options credited to capital

Choosing a model of the reporting entity: the FASB and the ASB

As part of its conceptual framework the FASB adopted the EM in the *Elements of Financial Statements* (FASB, 1985). The relative merits of PEEM and EM were however thoroughly re-examined in the context of accounting for financial instruments in the Discussion Memorandum, *Distinguishing between liability and equity instruments and accounting for instruments with characteristics of both* (FASB, 1990). Strong support was expressed in favour of the EM. Hence, the conceptual definitions of equity and liabilities set out in the *Elements of Financial Statements* were retained.

In the UK the process of establishing a conceptual framework for financial accounting principles began much later. However, in the discussion draft of the ASB's *Elements of financial statements* (ASB, 1992) there is evidence of confusion between the PEEM and the EM. The view is expressed in para., 62 (ASB, 1992) that when accounting for transactions between new owners and pre-existing owners, differences between the consideration received and the value of the equity issued should reflect the gain or loss to the pre-existing entity. This is consistent with the PEEM. In effect, transactions between new and pre-existing owners are to be accounted for as if they were liabilities. This is however contradicted in the section defining equity interest. Warrants to subscribe for shares are examples of a transaction between existing shareholders and third parties. In para., 47 (ASB,1995) these are classified as equity securities on the grounds that no obligation exists to transfer resources of the entity. This view, is however, consistent only with the EM and requires a transaction between pre-existing equity and those granted rights to subscribe for new shares to be accounted for as if it were equity.

The internal inconsistency between choice of model and definitions of the elements of the financial statements is not repeated in the subsequent publication of the Statement of Principles (SoP) exposure draft (ASB,1995). Adherence to the PEEM is unequivocally stated (ASB, 1995, 3.52). However, the definition and discussion of a liability is vague and unsatisfactory in that it fails to reflect, for the PEEM, the broader definition necessary to include transactions between new and pre-existing owners. In fact the definition provided does not specify the entity to which it relates and is consistent with the narrower view of liabilities in the EM.

If accounting regulators go so far as to require application of a particular model of the reporting entity for the measurement of income then the model ought to be clearly specified. Indeed, this is the purpose of the definitions of the elements of financial statements. There is scope for the ASB to do more to heighten awareness about the different models. In particular, the reasons for adopting the PEEM ought to be clearly identified. To date, the ASB has provided no leadership in promoting a debate in the UK about the relative merits of different models of the reporting entity. Only a single alternative has been presented. The impression given is that this choice has not been fully considered, particularly in the light of the unclear definitions of liabilities and equity provided in the recent drafts of the SoP.

Accounting for share-based compensation in practice

Accounting for share-based compensation provides an ideal opportunity to evaluate Baxter's view that regulators ought not to pronounce on theoretical concepts. The ingredients of choosing among models, appropriate measurement methods and proposals to significantly reduce income combine to create an explosive mixture. Following the 1990 Discussion Memorandum the decision to retain the EM and not to change the definitions of equity and debt cleared the way for the FASB to consider how to account for share-based compensation. The proposed accounting treatment, set out in the exposure draft (FASB, 127-c,1993), accorded strictly with the EM. Share-based compensation was to be measured by its fair value at the date of grant and accrued as an expense over the service period.

A particular merit claimed for this recommendation was that the charge for share-based compensation did not depend on the method of funding. However, the differential impact on income of costs of dilution arising from the method of settlement was not evaluated. Rather, these differences, although acknowledged, were taken as given because they are consistent with the EM. Thus, fair value on the date of grant is applied to equity instruments, while for liabilities, compensation expense is fair value on the date of exercised i.e. S_T-X. In this respect the dictates of the model were accepted uncritically. The fears of Baxter appear to be justified. Adoption of a specific model in the hands of the regulators seems to have served as a straight jacket. Critical evaluation of the full impact on income from application of the chosen model was inhibited.

In the eventual standard (FAS 123, FASB, 1995, para., 58) reaction to these proposals was described as "extraordinarily controversial"[8]. The response of the FASB in FAS 123 was to encourage companies to adopt its earlier proposals but it did not require that these be followed. Instead, companies were permitted to disclose the pro-forma effect of share-based compensation on income and earnings per share.

The ASB has not addressed the issue of accounting for share based compensation. However, in response to public concern about accountability for directors' remuneration the Urgent Issues Task Force (Abstract 10, ASB,1994) considered the issue of disclosure of directors' options. Comprehensive disclosure, in excess of statutory requirements, of directors' options was recommended. This response is accordance with views of Baxter. Information is made available without the need to specify measurement methods or identify the concept of income which is to be applied. In the light of the problems encountered by the FASB the cautious approach of the ASB may be more appropriate, at this stage, than the prescriptive model driven approach of the FASB.

Recommendations

The recommendations on accounting for share based remuneration proposed in this paper take no account of "political" reaction by the preparers of financial statements. Rather they are drawn from the principles of accounting set out in this essay. The proposed solution has the merit of producing identical measures of income under the PEEM and EM independent of different methods of settlement.

The first proposal is consistent with the analysis and recommendations of the FASB in its exposure draft (FASB, 127-c, 1993) and eventual standard. Irrespective of the funding method, compensation expense ought to be based on the fair value of the financial instruments at the date of grant. Following the insight of Lindahl, compensation expense should be restricted to the date of grant *ex ante* value of options. This value reflects the best estimate, at the date of grant, of the cost to the company of the award irrespective of the method of settlement. Subsequent valuation changes, ought to be accounted for as *ex post* windfall effects and excluded from the calculation of income. Thus, when an option instrument is either forfeited, lapses or is exercised, gains or losses suffered by pre-existing shareholders are recognised in financial statements as a matter of display and accounted for as capital adjustments. In the UK context this would be reported in the Reconciliation of Movements on Shareholders' Funds (FRS3, ASB, 1992).

To ensure managerial accountability for issues of equity which dilute the interests of pre-existing shareholders all new issues ought to be accounted for at fair value. Thus, even in the context of the EM, the full cost of dilution associated with the exercise of share based compensation will be reported irrespective of the type of financing instruments employed.

To accommodate these recommendations the conventional definitions applicable to liabilities and non-reciprocal transfers involving owners in the A-L=E model must be changed. The changes apply to the PEEM and the EM. In the case of liabilities, valuation changes *ex post* the date of an exchange transaction are classified as non-reciprocal transfers and are accounted for as capital adjustments. In the EM, new issues of equity are issued at fair value and, to provide comparability with liabilities, changes in value are recognised as they occur.

Notes:

1.   These authors, however, held very different views on the most desirable type of regulatory framework. Solomons favoured a normative deductive model based on the interests of investors. This model has been adopted by the FASB. Stamp advocated a more flexible approach designed to satisfy a wider constituency of users of financial statements.

2.   Non-reciprocal transfers do not commit the entity to deliver resources. For example, when capital is contributed, owners have no legal right to demand dividends.

3.   Definitions for the variables and option pricing terminology referred to in the text are provided in Figure 2.

4.   For simplicity, the option pricing formulae are those applicable to non-dividend paying stocks. Refinements of the Black and Scholes (1973) option pricing formula to reflect anticipated payment of dividends are presented in Hull (1989, p.135).

5.   Valuation of conventional transferable options is based on the full term, as it is normally advantageous to hold transferable options until they expire. The tradable value of the option before expiry will incorporate the remaining time value. Employee options are non-transferrable. Exercise before expiry of the full term terminates the exposure of the company and reduces the cost of the option. For this reason the FASB (FAS, 1995, para., 169) recommends that valuation be based on the expected life of the option.

6.   Exercise date measurement is generally considered relevant only for liability instruments.

7.   Strictly, measuring the windfall loss by S_t-X-c_o requires that the risk free rate of interest is zero. If the difference is material then a simple adjustment can be made.

8.   It was also observed that "The debate on accounting for stock based compensation unfortunately became so divisive that it threatened the Board's future working relationship with some of its constituents. Eventually, the nature of the debate threatened the future of accounting standards in the private sector." (FAS 123, FASB, 1995, para., 60).

References

American Accounting Association, (1994) "Response to Exposure Draft, Accounting for Stock Based Compensation", Accounting Horizons, Vol 8, 2, pp 114-116.

Accounting Standards Board, (1992) "Reporting Financial Performance", Financial Reporting Standard 3, ASB London.

_____, (1994) "Disclosure of directors' share options", Urgent Issues Task Force, Abstract 10, ASB London.

Accounting Standards Board, (1995) "Statement of Principles for Financial Reporting", Exposure Draft, ASB, London.

Baxter, W T, (1953) "Recommendations on accounting theory", The Accountant, October; reprinted in Collected Papers on Accounting, Arno Press, 1978, New York.

Black, F, and M Scholes, (1973) "The pricing of options and corporate liabilities", Journal of Political Economy, pp 637-659.

Financial Accounting Standards Board, (1985) "Elements of financial statements", Statement of Financial Accounting Concepts Number 6, FASB, Norwalk, Conn.

_____, (1990) "Distinguishing between liability and equity instruments and accounting for instruments with characteristics of both", Discussion Memorandum, FASB, Norwalk, Conn.

_____, (1993) "Accounting for Stock Based Compensation, Proposed Statement of Financial Accounting Standard, 127-c, FASB, Norwalk, Conn.

Financial Accounting Standards Board, (1995) "Accounting for Stock Based Compensation", Financial Accounting Standard 123, FASB, Norwalk, Conn.

Fisher, I, (1906) The Nature of Capital and Income, Macmillan.

Hicks, J R, (1939) Value and Capital, Oxford University Press.

Hull, J, (1989) Options Futures and other Derivative Securities, Prentice-Hall, Eaglewood Cliffs, N J.

Kaldor, N, (1955) "The Concept of Income in Economic Theory", An Expenditure Tax, Allen and Unwin, pp 54-78.

Lindahl, E, (1939) Studies in the Theory of Money and Capital, Allen and Unwin.

Paton, W.A. (1922) Accounting Theory: with special reference to the corporate enterprise, Ronald Press, New York, reprinted by Scholars Book Co., 1973, Texas.

Schmidt, F, (1921) Die organische Bilanz im Rahmen der Wirtschaft, Gloeckner.

Solomons, D. (1983) "The political implications of accounting and standard setting", Accounting and Business Research, 50, Spring, pp.107-118.

Stamp, E. (1980) "Corporate Reporting: Its Future Evolution", Canadian Institute of Chartered Accountants.

THE 'AMORTIZED COST' BASIS FOR FIXED-INTEREST INVESTMENTS: A NOTE ON ECONOMIC, ACTUARIAL AND ACCOUNTING CONCEPTS OF VALUE AND INCOME

Joanne Horton and Richard Macve

Introduction

'Accountants have been adept at arranging the figures in alternative ways that may or may not suggest income...... It does not get us out of the wood to call some gains "capital"......... these items may nonetheless seem in other respects to be income. There are, however, two exceptions:

(1)   Suppose a testamentary trust starts with a capital £100,000 and invests this in irredeemable fixed-interest securities to earn £6,000 a year, the market rate of interest then being 6 per cent. Later, the rate drops to 5 per cent, i.e. the value of the securities rises to £120,000. In one sense, there is here a gain of £20,000. If, however, the trustees now sold £20,000 of the securities and paid out the proceeds, future revenue would drop to only £5,000 a year; the recipients of income would be delighted this year but very dismayed next year. So, where gain is due to change in the market rate of interest, at least part of it may usefully be excluded from some definitions of income.

(2)   Where there is gain in money terms but not real terms.'

(Baxter, 1984, pp 27-8; 1975, p 25)

It is now over twenty years since Baxter (1975) set out fully the roles of revaluation and general price level adjustments for accounting in a period of inflation and over fifty years since Hicks (1946)[1] wrote what is, at least among accountants, probably the best known discussion of 'income' (including the effects of interest rate changes and inflation). With the publication of the ASB's Exposure Draft of the chapters of its Statement of Principles (1995) there is a widespread view that the Board is moving inexorably, albeit gradually (by an 'evolutionary' process (para. 5.37)), towards a fundamental shift from historical cost as the basis for asset and liability measurement and the determination of periodic income (or 'earnings') to 'current values' (e.g. Ernst & Young, 1996). While its choice of valuation basis may be eclectic, theoretically the Board favours 'value to the business' (ASB, 1995, 5.35), a concept for which Baxter has frequently and elegantly argued under the label of 'deprival value' (e.g. Baxter, 1975; c.f. Baxter, 1994). The ASB, in FRS3 (1993, para.27), has also promoted the 'statement of total recognised gains and losses' (henceforward 'STRGL') to be a primary financial statement to display those gains and losses (such as unrealized gains on fixed asset revaluations) which complement the earnings that are reported in the profit and loss account (hereafter 'P&L'). Moreover, the ASB has reinforced the significance of the STRGL by requiring that, once gains have been recognised there (but outside the P&L), they cannot subsequently be recognised again (e.g. when 'realised') by being 'transferred' into P&L at that stage[2]. In this respect the ASB has moved further than the FASB in the USA, which also requires certain gains and losses to be taken (temporarily) straight to owners' equity, by-passing the income statement, but in the majority of cases recognises them in the income statement as 'earnings' in a later accounting period (Johnson and Reither, 1995)[3].

Even if the adoption of current values by the ASB is in practice likely to be only piecemeal, a prime candidate is stock-market investments and ED55 of the ASC (issued July 1990) proposed 'marking to market' as the basis for readily marketable investments held as current assets, both for balance sheet valuation and for the determination of 'realised profits' in the profit and loss account, and, although recommending cost for fixed asset investments, allowed their revaluation to current value (but with the gains taken to revaluation reserve)[4]. However, the exposure draft still lies on the table, as the proposal for marking to market languishes under the prohibition in the Companies Act 1985, Schedule 4, para. 22, against the valuation of current assets at more than 'purchase price or production cost' unless the revaluation surplus is taken to revaluation reserve.

Although stock exchange investments are perhaps the most obvious candidate for 'marking to market' where held as current assets, and for regular revaluation where held as fixed assets, one case, namely redeemable fixed-interest securities, gives rise to particular conceptual difficulties. ED55 included such securities under its general proposals but stated (para. 35) that, where such securities are not marked to market nor revalued to current value, they should be accounted for on the basis of 'amortized cost', whereby any premium or discount on redemption value is systematically amortized over the period to redemption, gradually reducing or increasing the balance sheet value and reporting as income in each period the 'redemption yield' on the security.

The amortized cost basis for accounting for fixed-interest securities is the mirror-image of the 'effective yield' method for fixed-interest debt liabilities. Thus the Revenue authorities in the USA have been concerned that there should be parity of treatment between assessing taxable income from investments and giving relief for allowable expenses on borrowings (e.g. Macve, 1984). Recently in the UK the Inland Revenue has altered the basis of taxation of gilts and bonds (with effect from 1 April 1996) so that for corporate[5] investors and borrowers the distinction between 'income' and 'capital' will be eliminated, and the total return, whether by way of interest or of profit on redemption or disposal, will be taxed, with losses correspondingly obtaining tax relief. Periodic tax assessment will be based on the figures appearing in companies accounts provided these are either on an accruals basis[6] or a mark-to-market basis.[7]

It is unclear whether these new tax requirements will now be affected by any change in accounting treatment from that currently required under FRS3 (under which profits or losses on disposal of investments by investors or on redemption of debentures by borrowers are taken to profit and loss account). If the ASB's new proposal in the draft Statement of Principles (i.e. that gains and losses on fixed assets, including investments held as fixed assets, be taken to STRGL and excluded from P&L) is confirmed, this would logically lead to a corresponding revision of FRS3. (This potential change will be discussed further below.) The recent SORP for investment trust companies (ITCs) (AITM, 1995), which requires 'market value' for all their quoted investments, does not treat fixed-interest investments differently in this respect from other quoted investments. But all investments of investment trusts are 'fixed assets' and ITCs share the common feature that any 'capital gains' must, by their constitutions, be excluded from their P&L ('revenue account') and from distributable profits, so that all gains and losses on revaluation will go to STRGL. As for the P&L treatment, the SORP requires the amortized cost basis for calculating the 'revenue profits' from ITCs' fixed-interest securities.

Certain other regulatory requirements appear to regard the amortized cost basis as effectively an alternative way of applying requirements for current valuation/marking to market, that is as, if not more, appropriate for this kind of investment. Thus the Regulations implementing the EU Insurance Accounts Directive in the UK (SI1993/3246) provide (para.22) that insurance companies' investments (which are not classified into 'fixed' and 'current' assets) should generally be stated at current value (with the unrealized gains and losses normally being either required or permitted to be included in the profit and loss account, unlike those of most other kinds of companies (Horton & Macve, 1995, Chapter 10)). But, in the case of 'debt securities and other fixed-income securities', para. 24 provides that they may either be valued at current value or on the amortized cost basis[8]. Moreover, para. 24(7) takes up the option allowed under the Directive (Article 55 (2)) that, where securities valued on the amortized cost basis are sold before maturity, and the proceeds are used to purchase other fixed-interest securities, insurance companies may spread the 'profit' or 'loss' on sale uniformly over the period remaining until maturity of the original investment.[9]

In the USA FAS115 (FASB, 1993), which applies to the investments held by all kinds of enterprises,[10] distinguishes three kinds of investments:

(1) Debt securities intended to be held to maturity, 'hold-to-maturity securities', which are reported at amortized cost.

(2) Debt and equity securities bought and held principally for the purpose of selling them in the near term - 'trading securities' - which are reported at fair value, with the changes in value reported in the income statement (i.e. marked to market).

(3) Other debt and equity securities - 'available-for-sale securities' - which are reported at fair value, with the changes in value taken direct to owners' equity and not reported in earnings in the income statement until the securities are sold.

In the case of hold-to-maturity securities there should normally be no holding gains or losses as the difference between purchase cost and maturity proceeds will be amortized systematically using the 'effective interest' method (c.f. Macve, 1984). If there are any realised gains or losses they are reported in earnings. In Canada, fluctuations in the value of insurance companies' portfolio investments are normally smoothed both by using a 'moving average market method' for valuation of equities and for recognition of realised and unrealized gains and losses, and by using amortized cost as the basis of valuation for fixed-term investments with any realised gains and losses amortized over the remaining term to maturity of the investments sold (i.e. they are regarded as resulting from changes in interest rates and are thereby matched against the rates of return earned on the reinvested funds). The balance of any deferred realised gains or losses is presented in the balance sheet outside shareholders' equity (CICA, 1988).[11] (Such a balance would not appear to fit any of the definitions of 'elements of financial statements' given in the conceptual frameworks of standard setting bodies (e.g. FASB, 1980; IASC, 1989; ASB, 1995).)

So even just within the English-speaking world there is a variety of practice in accounting for fixed-interest investments in different circumstances. Our objective in the remainder of this paper is to explore the use of 'amortized cost' and why it is widely regarded as the most appropriate basis for dealing with fixed-interest investments, whether short or long-term, even in contexts where other investments are being accounted for at market value rather than historical cost. A more satisfactory approach, that would satisfy better the conventional objectives of financial accounting and reporting, would appear to be to combine current market valuation in the balance sheet with income determination on the 'amortized cost' basis, at least for long-term investments (e.g. as recommended in the ITC SORP). However, this raises a fundamental issue as to the intended role of the STRGL which has not yet been considered by ASB, and which has potential implications for accounting for fixed assets more generally.

In discussing these issues contrasts will be drawn between the approaches traditionally adopted by accountants and by members of another profession which has a primary responsibility for assessing the long-term performance of investments - the actuaries. There has recently been extensive debate of the issues relating to the measurement of performance of life insurance business (traditionally the actuaries' domain). The debate has stalled and a major hurdle has been inability to resolve how investment performance should be reported. The progress of that debate (e.g. Horton & Macve, 1995) may shed some light on why the issues that arise in investment accounting in all kinds of businesses are so intractable.

The remainder of the paper is structured as follows: In section (1) we consider the rationale for the amortized cost basis in the light of the conceptual difficulties that arise for income measurement from changes in the rate of interest, and briefly explore the implications of the alternative approaches to income measurement under these conditions as set out by Hicks (1946) and Paish (1940).[12] In section (2), we review the recent proposals of the ASB as to the basis for allocation of gains and losses between P&L and STRGL and argue that the ASB's draft Statement of Principles (like other standard setters' conceptual frameworks) ignores the issue of whether there are any changes in ownership interest[13] that are not 'gains and losses' but are merely arithmetic consequences of the double-entry articulation of balance-sheet and P&L, an articulation which, in itself, carries no economic or business significance (e.g. Macve, 1989).[14] The ASB's attempt to rely on rigorous balance sheet concepts in order to determine periodic income not only goes against much traditional accounting practice, but is also hard to reconcile with actuarial views of the nature and emergence of 'surplus' from long-term insurance business activities.[15] In section (3), we therefore review some relevant actuarial literature and consider the proposals in the draft revised ABI SORP (1995).

In **conclusion** we argue that, while the merits of market value based accounting for listed stock exchange investments are clear, they are not sufficient to resolve the issue of how much of the change in investment values during a period is to be regarded as income of that period, e.g. in measuring performance. On this issue the actuarial literature provides a valuable additional dimension to the accounting debate over income recognition[16], which has implications for the adequacy of the ASB's Statement of Principles as a basis for standard setting.

(1) The amortized cost basis

By 'locking in' the original anticipated yield on the acquisition/issue of a fixed-interest security the investor/borrower is insulated from the effect of variations in the prevailing rate of interest during its life and the amortized cost method reflects this 'locking-in' in its reporting of income. But this gives rise to a number of practical and conceptual accounting problems:[17]

- While Hicks (1946) preferred his 'No. 2' approximation to the central concept of income, which focusses on the maintainable earnings (here the annual amount to give the redemption yield), Paish (1940) argued that individuals' preferences as between 'capital value' and 'maintainable annual receipts' would vary so that one could not say in abstract terms how much of any capital gain or loss from a change in interest rates should be regarded as 'income'. 'Long-term' investors (e.g. pensioners or pension funds on their behalf) might be concerned primarily with maintainable income; other investors might be more concerned with redeemable capital value, either at maturity at a fixed horizon or from day to day (e.g. to provide funds for emergencies). Most individuals would have complex motives for investment. By extension, the 'income' of companies (representing the collectivities of their individual shareholders) could only be given any operational meaning in so far as it is constructed through social convention.

- Particular difficulties arise if redeemable fixed-interest investments are sold before maturity, when interest rates have changed since acquisition. There are incentives to manipulate reported earnings if the resulting 'gains' and 'losses' (i.e. the differences between book value and sales proceeds) are reported as income or earnings. Thus the background discussion to FAS 115 (FASB, 1993) noted the opportunity for 'gains trading' by selecting which securities to sell in order to report realised holding gains in earnings while not having to recognise in the same way concurrent holding losses on securities not sold. The two dissenting Board members refer to the fact that 'An impressive amount of empirical evidence indicates that many financial institutions have engaged in that behaviour' (para 11).

133

The traditional alternatives to recognising the realisation gains or losses in earnings are either to treat them as direct adjustments to equity capital (e.g. as in ITCs) or to roll them forward over the remaining period to maturity of the original investments (e.g. CICA, 1998). Neither alternative is readily justifiable within the terms of standard-setters' statements of concepts/principles (e.g. ASB, 1995, Chapter 3).[18]

- Changes in value (i.e. in the rate of interest demanded by investors) may result from a change in the perceived riskiness of the security. This will not normally apply in the case of gilts (apart from inflation risk) but may be a major factor in the case of corporate bonds. In so far as such changes can be identified they would appear to be a 'real' gain or loss (for further discussion see footnote 22 below).

(2) The ASB's STRGL

The ASB currently proposes (1995, 6.27-28) that 'gains and losses on those assets and liabilities that are held on a continuing basis primarily in order to enable the entity's operations to be carried out are reported in the statement of total recognised gains and losses, and not in the profit and loss account. All other gains and losses are reported in the profit and loss account'. Thus gains and losses on fixed assets (whether realised or unrealised) will appear in STRGL.[19]

It is noted (6.29) that the components of total recognised gains and losses for different entities will exhibit differing characteristics in terms of continuity or recurrence, stability, risk and reliability. The relative importance of the different components of total recognised gains and losses will, therefore, vary among entities.

For long term investment based entities, such as ITCs, the relative importance of gains and losses from revaluation of securities will be high. For ITCs, taking such gains and losses to STRGL (as is also recommended in the new ITC SORP (AITM, 1995)), on the basis that their investments are long-term 'infrastructure', also satisfies the legal requirements to keep 'capital' gains and losses outside their P&L account. For short-term investment based entities, such as market makers, for whom their investments are 'trading stock', it will be consistent with these proposals for their revaluation gains and losses to be taken to P&L ('marked to market')[20].

Insurance companies are a more difficult case: while much of the core of their investment may be 'long-term', investments may be regarded as being 'realised' (even if only notionally) to meet policyholder claims (including 'terminal bonuses' on with-profits life policies, which aim to reflect investment performance over the policy term (e.g. Horton and Macve, 1995)). Correspondingly the Companies Act (following the EU Insurance Accounts Directive) does not classify their investments as either 'fixed' or 'current'. The issue of how much of their gains and losses from revaluation of investments should therefore be regarded as arising on 'infrastructure' (and taken to STRGL) and how much as arising from 'trading' (and taken to P&L) is correspondingly more complex.

By extension, the same situation arises for 'ordinary companies' that hold an investment portfolio, maybe for a variety of reasons. As defined by ASB (1995, 6.27) they may be 'held on a continuing basis primarily in order to enable the entity's operations to be carried out' (e.g. what were traditionally called 'trade investments'), but they may also be the currently selected medium for disposal of surplus funds, being turned over in accordance with the dictates of treasury management. The FASB's FAS115 (1993) acknowledges the relevance of classifying investments as far as possible according to investment intention, and management intention would have to determine the classification of gains and losses set out under para 6.27-28 of the ASB's draft Statement of Principles. However, while this would appear to be appropriate for the purposes of income measurement, it seems anomalous that balance sheet values of investments should vary according to investment intention and that the same listed security could be valued on different bases - as is currently required by FAS115 - e.g. at amortized cost for the amount intended to be held to maturity and at market value for the amount regarded as 'available for sale' or 'trading'. Simplicity, clarity and comparability (as well as reduction of manipulation)[21] would favour reporting all holdings at market value.

The ASB's proposal that STRGL should receive those gains and losses that relate to 'fixed asset' investments also glosses over the fact that there are several different kinds of revaluation gains and losses being dealt with here, at least one of which may be argued not to be a gain or loss at all. In the case of equity investments changes in their value may reflect one or all of a change in the expected dividends they can pay (i.e. a change in the maintainable annual level of cash flow and so unambiguously a gain or loss), or in the riskiness of those dividends (which would also appear to be unambiguously a gain or loss)[22] or in the capitalisation rate (e.g. due to a change in the current or expected future rate of interest, where the amount of any gain or loss is, as Paish (1940) argued, essentially ambiguous (see further Macve & Jackson, 1991, chapter 1)). For the purposes of this discussion we will therefore classify the first two kinds of changes as 'cash flow changes' and the second as 'interest rate changes'. To carry gains and losses from both kinds of changes to STRGL is, in the context of the ASB's Statement of Principles where STRGL is a primary performance statement, to assert that they are both 'really' gains and losses, albeit of a kind not reported in P&L. By contrast the 'traditional' view has placed more emphasis on the interpretation that neither kind of change gives rise to 'real' gains and losses (so they cannot be reported in P&L), either because they are 'unrealised'[23] or because they are 'capital' (or both) - they are one of a number of miscellaneous items traditionally taken to 'reserve' (Ernst & Young, 1996, p.6).[24]

While it is consistent with the rest of the ASB's draft Statement of Principles, and with the arguments of those accounting theorists who have supported the reporting of current values in balance sheets and of 'holding gains' in income (e.g. Solomons, 1989), to promote the recognition of gains in STRGL as comprising part of the primary presentation of a company's performance, the change in emphasis from the traditional view is made the stronger by virtue of continuing not to distinguish those gains and losses arising from changes in the rate of interest from those arising from changes in anticipated cash flows. Conceptually, at least, there is a middle way, which would acknowledge as an element of what the FASB calls 'comprehensive' income (Johnson & Reither, 1995) and include in STRGL the gains that Hicks and Paish regard as being unambiguously income, while regarding those arising from changes in the rate of interest as needing to be distinguished (approximately in line with Paish's analysis - see Macve and

Jackson, 1991, Ch.1) into those arising in respect of 'current asset investments' (also properly included in P&L as income, as under 'marking to market'[25]) and those arising in respect of 'fixed asset investments' (which should be excluded from both P&L and STRGL and regarded as merely the double-entry arithmetic adjustment needed in order to maintain the balance sheet identity between net assets and ownership interest).

How would this approach deal with the 'realised' gains and losses that arise when fixed asset investments are sold? Under the ASB's current proposals these too would be reported in STRGL[26]. If those resulting from changes in the rate of interest could be identified (as they can with less difficulty in the case of fixed-interest investments[27]) then these gains and losses should similarly be segregated and be regarded as part of the 'arithmetic' adjustment, reflecting the investment intention. This adjustment would be reported directly as a change in ownership interest rather than in STRGL.[28] This implies that the approach advocated in Canada (and allowed in the UK Companies Act) for insurance companies' fixed-interest investments, whereby the gain or loss on disposal is 'spread forward', may be seen as essentially an alternative way of making this adjustment.

(3) Actuarial ideas and recent proposals for insurance investment accounting

The establishment of with-profits life insurance in the UK[29] onto a sound footing in the middle of the nineteenth century required the acceptance of actuarial principles by company managements and regulators (Horton and Macve, 1994; c.f. Alborn, 1994). The actuaries' professional concerns have traditionally been principally directed to the sound financial management of life companies, influenced in particular by considerations of equity between policyholders and above all by the need to maintain long-term solvency for policyholder protection.[30] Their recognition of a life company's profit ('surplus') has essentially been a financial decision about the appropriate pattern of its release over time rather than a measurement of the 'true' situation from year to year (e.g. Redington, 1952; Cox & Storr-Best, 1963; Skerman, 1968). Conservatism has been endemic. Even when actuaries have argued for more realistic bases of valuation, they have been cautious about the dangers of making them public for fear of unduly or prematurely raising policyholders' expectations.[31]

Actuaries have also traditionally shown little interest in accounting problems.[32] They have tended to see accountants as concerned primarily with accuracy and with verifiable facts about the past, whereas their own skills are in applying statistical estimation to look to the future in making judgements about equity, rate of distribution and solvency (e.g. Coutts, 1926, pp 159-60: c.f. p187; Jenkins Committee, 1963, p.111; Hall, 1966, p.367; Smith, 1973, p.255). For these purposes it is ultimately only the anticipated balance between future income and outgo that is relevant, and 'valuations' are only relevant insofar as they assist judgement about that anticipated balance (c.f. Dyson and Exley, 1995), so that changes in the current market values of assets may often be regarded as of relatively little significance (e.g. White & Holmes, 1939; Suttie, 1944; Skerman, 1966, p.83; 1968, pp 72-3; Scholey, 1969, pp 410-2; Bews et al., 1975; Fine et al., 1988). The weight of articles in the Journal of the Institute of Actuaries and its successor the British Actuarial Journal[33] reflects their primary professional interest in the insurance implications, issues and statistics relating to mortality and investment returns (including the impacts of taxation and, more recently, of the use of computers). When confronted with accounting issues they have, at least officially, argued for retention of the traditional flexibility of 'secret reserve' accounting and, at least in the past, against 'potentially misleading' disclosures of investment values.[34]

A classic treatment is that of Pegler (1948) nearly 50 years ago who, in restating the principles of insurance company investment and the interdependence of asset and liability valuation, discussed two issues:

(a)   How much of the disclosed surplus may be regarded as disposable?

(b)   How should that part of the surplus which is not disposable be treated in the published accounts?

In Pegler's view 'the second problem is the simpler and will be treated first. It is a question of book-keeping which cannot in the long run affect the profit or solvency of the office, and its solution is therefore purely a matter of expediency.'

The actuary could either

(1)   create a hidden reserve by writing down book value of assets

or (2)   publish full market values and set up a reserve in the published accounts or increase the undivided surplus carried forward

or (3)   use some combination of (1) and (2)

Pegler notes that (1) appears to be 'officially tolerated, in view of the exclusion of life offices from the provisions of the recent (i.e. 1948) Companies Act regarding hidden reserves' (p.192). It leaves the actuary free to draw on the reserve in future without disclosing this or having to justify it to policyholders or shareholders.

On the other hand (2) shows strength - but also any subsequent depreciation and need to 'draw on reserves' when they are used for the purposes for which they are designed. Less intelligent members of public may misunderstand (e.g. if other offices are not revealing draw-down). 'In practice the choice must depend on the amount of surplus to be reserved and the circumstances obtaining at the time, but I would suggest that notwithstanding the dictum "freedom with publicity" the traditional bias of the actuary in favour of concealing at least a part of the strength of his reserves is, on the whole, a healthy one' (p.193).

In Pegler's view, how much surplus to reserve is the major problem, and a much more difficult question. Most of it comes from appreciation in security values but it is a fallacy that investments cannot depreciate below cost - so leaving them at cost is no answer. It is also a fallacy that realised profit is any more real than current, ephemeral, arbitrary market value. For this purpose 'capital' appreciation is not sacrosanct - the distinction between capital and income is almost meaningless. In this context amortized cost is not much help, for Pegler argues that: 'In the case of redeemable fixed-interest securities, one may perhaps make some transfer between capital and income on the basis, say, of the original assumptions as to yield on which the security was bought. Such an assumption is somewhat arbitrary, but is mathematically possible. In the case of equities it is difficult to see on what principle any such distinction can be made.' (p.193).

The essence, Pegler argues, is to reserve[36] for the risk of assets falling more than liabilities. So depreciation in capital from a rise in rate of interest can, if assets and liabilities are approximately 'matched' as regards outstanding life, largely be ignored. However offices are always reluctant to raise the valuation rate to be applied to liabilities, so they need to be able to absorb the effect of e.g. a 0.5% rise on the market value of fixed interest securities. But depreciation from fall in future income earning power of assets cannot be offset by reducing liabilities, and Pegler noted that 'good class equities have fallen' about 50% over the trade cycle. So this problem, he considers, needs serious consideration[36].

To the actuary therefore valuation has traditionally been a tool in long-term financial management. The last two decades, however, have seen a the emergence of a new emphasis. While maintaining due regard for the 'reasonable expectations of policyholders and potential policyholders', as required by the Insurance Companies Acts (e.g. Franklin & Woodhead, 1980, ch.10), actuaries have shown increasing concern with the interests of shareholders (e.g. Benjamin, 1972, p.235), discussing, for example, valuations for the purpose of purchasing companies (Bangert, 1973), demutualisations (Needleman & Westall, 1991) and the profitability of new business (Smart, 1977). In parallel, and perhaps reflecting the emergence in the British Isles of Statements of Standard Accounting Practice in 1971 (e.g. Smith, 1973, p 290) and the aftermath of the failure of the V&G and other companies in the early 1970s (Franklin & Woodhead, 1980, ch.10; Harte & Macve, 1991), actuaries have also shown an increasing interest in accounting issues and in the differences between actuarial and accountancy concepts and approaches to valuation and profit determination (e.g. Bangert, 1973, pp 157-9[37]; Benjamin, 1976) and in questions of improved disclosure of insurance companies' affairs (e.g. Smith, 1973; Burrows & Whitehead, 1987; Lyon, 1988). Nevertheless, some of the major accounting issues, such as inflation accounting, have bypassed insurance companies.[38]

The actuaries, aware that the valuation methods used for solvency purposes under the DTI Regulations are very conservative and understate the performance of a growing life fund (even though full disclosure of market values of investments is now required), have developed new approaches such as 'embedded value', 'accruals' profits and 'achieved profits', using more realistic assumptions, to give a better estimate of the value of the shareholders' interest in the business in force and of the performance of the company (especially in generating new business) (Salmon & Fine, 1991; Horton & Macve, 1995) as well as for profit testing, planning and control (Goford, 1985; c.f. Anderson & Binns, 1957). A new interest in life accounting profits among proprietary companies has also recently been spurred by the greater competition in the financial services industry following the Financial Services Act, 1986, including an increasing number of takeovers of insurance companies by banks and conglomerates.

The aim of these new approaches is to reflect more realistically the pattern of the profit on a life-policy or other long-term insurance contract and thereby give a better measure of managerial performance and of the profitability of management actions and decisions. The debate over the new methods (e.g. Adams and Scott, 1994) has brought out once again the fundamental differences between the actuaries' approach, essentially forward looking in assessing a company's financial position, and the accountants' approach, which, at least as understood by the EC Commission, fundamentally looks backwards over each year's activity in assessing periodic performance (c.f. ICAEW, 1992).

One of the major issues outstanding is that of how to deal with investment gains and losses. A number of major companies adopt a policy of 'smoothing' investment results e.g. by taking a five year moving average. However, both the ASB and the DTI are concerned that this practice is unacceptable given the normal requirements of accounting standards and of interpreting legal requirements (see e.g. ABI, 1995).

We do not discuss here the full range of issues relating to 'smoothing' of equity or property investment returns[39] (see e.g. Horton & Macve, 1995, pp 245-262) but consider those issues that arise primarily in relation to accounting for fixed-interest securities and their implications for other accounting problems. As noted above, although it is now normal practice in the UK, and is required by the valuation rules for solvency purposes in preparing the DTI returns, to value all investments at market value (and correspondingly to value actuarial liabilities for long-term business by reference to current rates of interest), flexibility is still allowed under the 1993 Regulations (SI1993/3246) to value fixed-interest securities at amortized cost in the financial statements prepared under the Companies Act.[40] But, even if market values are universally applied, it might to be permissible to spread holding gains and losses in a manner that has the same effect as using the amortized cost basis. The conceptual justification would be (as has been argued above) that, where fixed-interest investments are to be held to maturity (i.e. as fixed assets), the gains and losses on book values due to changes in interest rates are not to be regarded as real gains and losses.[41]

Thus, it would seem to be more helpful, while adopting market value for the balance sheet, to take the resulting gains and losses deemed to arise from changes in the rate of interest directly to the ownership interest, bypassing both P&L and STRGL.[42] This element of owners' interest would conceptually be closer to the 'deferred credits' and 'deferred debits' of the traditional 'matching' approach to profit measurement (e.g. Ernst & Young, 1996) than to any of the elements currently defined in the ASB's draft Statement of Principles (or other standard setters' conceptual frameworks). It would provide a temporary home for differences between changes in net asset values and recognised gains and losses - but in most cases should reverse as the changes in net asset values become 'real' gains and losses. Such a procedure would still satisfy the ASB's prohibition on 'double recognition' of gains and losses (e.g. first on revaluation in STRGL and then, as realised, in P&L) as these 'gains and losses' would originally bypass STRGL. Similar procedures could apply on disposal of a fixed interest security before maturity. The gain or loss would again bypass STRGL and P&L and be taken directly to the ownership interest - from where it could be amortized to P&L over the remaining term of the original security in order to bring the net yield on the replacement security back in line with that on the original security (as is required for Canadian insurance companies under CICA 1988 - and as is allowed for UK insurance companies by the Companies Act under the IAD (SI1993/3246, para 22)).

This approach would seem to be in line with Baxter's (1984) and Edwards and Bell's (1961) recommendations, e.g. for revalued fixed assets, whereby the realised cost savings / holding gains are fed into P&L to bring depreciation back to its historical cost level. So companies would account for both the old and new securities at market value with income yield shown initially as that currently prevailing, but with adjustment from the revaluation surplus (temporarily held in ownership interest) to bring the net yield back to the historical redemption yield on the old securities[43].

Implications and conclusions

The particular conceptual difficulties arising from changes in the rate of interest raise the question of whether the ASB's new approach to fixed assets more generally is appropriate (whereby any revaluations would be reported in STRGL and depreciation thereafter based on the revalued figure). Again it could be argued, in so far as

(a)   the value changes resulted from changes in capitalisation rates and

(b)   the assets were held for their long-term earning power,

that this element of any gains should be excluded from STRGL and taken direct to ownership interest - and that depreciation thereafter should be adjusted by systematic transfer from this 'deferred credit' to P&L in order to maintain the original level of earnings (ceteris paribus)[44]. However, as Baxter has argued (e.g. 1984, p.115), in the case of physical fixed assets such changes must for all practical purposes be ignored.

> `The only time when the specific-index case appears valid is when input appreciation
> is not due to change in expected net receipts, but in their capitalisation rate (p.111).
> Then the gain is so different from other forms of income that it might well be excluded
> or at least carefully segregated. But such gains seem likely to be rare, hard to
> distinguish, and harder to quantify. So we may doubt whether they deserve much space
> in a reform programme. '

But in the case of equity investments, especially where these are central to the business, as in an investment trust or insurance company, a case may be made for attempting to distinguish such changes in value from those due to changes in expected dividends[45]. In the case of fixed interest investments of course, the amount of such changes is much clearer provided changes in risk can be excluded (as with gilts). While ITCs have traditionally 'avoided' the problem by treating all investment gains as 'capital' and excluding them from income, their new SORP now follows FRS3 in taking all revaluation and realisation gains through STRGL as part of performance and they report a statistic for `total return per share' comprising both the `revenue' and `capital' elements (AITiM, 1995). Additional explanation may therefore now be needed by ITCs (e.g. in relation to their earnings per share calculations) to assist understanding of the special nature of these investment returns. In the case of insurance companies, they are now permitted to take all gains, realised and unrealised, to P&L (and are required to do so in the case of long term business investments) but the major with-profits offices still wish to smooth the returns.[46] One justification may be that, in so far as gains and losses are due to interest rate changes, and they are invested for the long term, the fluctuations in value are irrelevant to their performance.

In all these cases there is therefore a conflict between wanting to value the investments at market value and not wanting to report all the gains and losses through P&L or STRGL. This conflict could be resolved if companies could account for the relevant gains and losses by direct transfer to ownership interest. So, in the case of fixed-interest securities, the amortized cost basis could apply to the determination of income but not to the measurement of balance sheet value, and the market value fluctuations would bypass the performance statements. In this way the objectives of managers, actuaries and accountants may all be met.

From these considerations it is clear that, while the ASB, like other standard setters, has adopted the 'balance sheet' approach in developing its conceptual framework, thereby aiming to eliminate the 'deferred debits and credits' that result from the 'matching' approach (c.f. Ernst & Young, 1996), such determination of balance sheet values does not in itself give complete guidance on how `earnings' and `income' are to be measured. The concepts needed for establishing the principles of performance measurement cannot be founded solely on definitions and recognition criteria for assets and liabilities and measurement of changes in their value.[47] This is brought out particularly clearly where changes in value are due to interest rate changes. As we have argued, these still merit handling outside both STRGL and P&L in appraising performance, and this can be done at least for long-term fixed-interest investments if not for investments more generally. This is the `message' of the amortized cost basis and its continuing popularity reflects the underlying conceptual difficulties about income measurement for which it has traditionally offered a practical solution.

Moreover, if the `balance sheet approach' cannot resolve issues of income and performance measurement even in the case of marketable investments (where the case for balance sheet revaluation is strongest), it is therefore more dubious whether revaluations of other kinds of assets should be required. The ASB's proposed `evolutionary' approach should itself be regarded as a principle rather than a pragmatic, political compromise adopted to secure acceptance of its agenda (c.f. Ernst & Young, 1996; Zeff, 1996). The Statement of Principles needs to reflect these additional complexities, in the light of the variety of objectives and consequences of preparing accounts (Zeff, 1978), if it is to be of real value in guiding and developing improvements in accounting practice. A wholesale review of investment accounting, both within and outwith the financial services sector, would be a first step in helping to identify where the crucial difficulties lie.

Acknowledgements:

The assistance of the Assistant Librarian, Institute of Actuaries, Staple Inn, London WC1, and of the National Library of Wales, Aberystwyth is gratefully acknowledged. We thank Mark Tippett for his helpful comments on an earlier version. Part of the research for this paper has been undertaken with the aid of sponsorship from the Research Board of the Institute of Chartered Accountants in England & Wales and from KPMG Peat Marwick.

References

ABI (Association of British Insurers), Guidance on Accounting for Insurance Business, December, 1995

AITM (Association of Investment Trust Managers), SORP, Accounting for Investment Trusts, 1995

Adams, M.B., and Scott, C.N.W., `Realistic Reporting of Life Company Policy Liabilities and Profits', Journal of the Institute of Actuaries, 121, II (479), 1994, pp 441-458

Alborn, T.L., `A Calculating Profession: Victorian Actuaries among the Statisticians', Science in Context 7,3, 1994, pp 433-468

Anderson, J.L., `Notes on the Effect of Changes in Rates of Interest on the Bonus-Earning Power of an Office Paying a Uniform Compound Bonus', Transactions of the Faculty of Actuaries, 1944, pp 137-173

Anderson, J.L and Binns, J.D., 'The Actuarial Management of a Life Office', Journal of the Institute of Actuaries, 83, 1957, pp 112-52

ASB (Accounting Standards Board), FRS3, Reporting Financial Performance, 1993 (issued October, 1992; amended June, 1993)

ASB, Exposure Draft, Statement of Principles For Financial Reporting, November, 1995

ASB, Discussion Paper, Impairment of Tangible Fixed Assets, April, 1996

ASC (Accounting Standards Committee), Exposure Draft ED55, Accounting for Investments, July, 1990

Bangert, R.M., 'Valuation of a Life Assurance Company for Purchase', Journal of the Institute of Actuaries, 99, 1973, pp 131-70

Bank of England, Strips and New Instruments in the Gilt-Edged Market, May, 1995

Baxter, W.T., Inflation Accounting, McGraw-Hill, 1975

Baxter, W.T., Inflation Accounting, Philip Allan, 1984

Baxter, W.T., 'Asset and Liability Values', Accountancy, April, 1994, pp 135-7

Baxter, W.T., `Future Events - A Conceptual Study of their Significance for Recognition and Measurement, A Review Article', Accounting and Business Research, 26, 2, Spring 1996, pp 171-176

Benjamin, S., Discussion of 'Supervision of Insurance in the UK', Journal of the Institute of Actuaries, 98, 1972, pp 233-50

Benjamin, S., 'Profit and Other Financial Concepts in Insurance', Journal of the Institute of Actuaries, 103, 1976, pp 233-305

Bews, R.P., Seymour, P.A.C., Shaw, A.W.D. & Wales, F.R., 'Proposals for the Statutory Basis of Valuation of the Liabilities of Long-Term Insurance Business', Journal of the Institute of Actuaries, 102, 1975, pp 61-113

Bromwich, M., Financial Reporting, Information and Capital Markets, Pitman, 1992

Burrows, R.P. and Whitehead, G.H., 'The Determination of Life Office Appraisal Values', Journal of the Institute of Actuaries, 114, 1987, pp 411-465

CICA (Canadian Institute of Chartered Accountants) Handbook, Accounting Recommendations, Section 4210 on 'Life Insurance Enterprises - Specific Items', May 1988 (amended March 1990, March 1991).

Cohen Committee on Company Law Amendment: Discussion, Journal of the Institute of Actuaries, 73, 1947, pp.20-36

Coutts, C.R.V., 'On the Distribution of Life Profits', Journal of the Institute of Actuaries, 57, 1926, pp 159-91

Cox, P.R. and Storr-Best, R.H., 'Surplus: Two Hundred Years of Actuarial Advance', Journal of the Institute of Actuaries, 89, 1963, pp 19-60

Draper, P.R., McInnes, W.M., Marshall, A.P. and Pope. P.F., 'An Assessment of the Effective Annual Rate Method as a Basis for Making Accounting Allocations', Journal of Business Finance and Accounting, 20(1), 1993, pp 143-151

Dyson, A.C.L. and Exley, C.J., `Pension Fund Asset Valuation and Investment ', British Actuarial Journal, I, III, 1995, pp 471-557

Edey, H.C., 'Accounting principles and business reality', Accountancy, 74, November & December, 1963

Edwards, E.O and Bell, P.W., The Theory and Measurement of Business Income, Berkeley: University of California Press, 1961

Ernst & Young, Budget 95 Alert, Ernst & Young, London, 1995

Ernst & Young, The ASB's Framework: Time to Decide, Ernst & Young, London, February, 1996.

FASB (US Financial Accounting Standards Board), Statement of Financial Accounting Concepts No. 3, Elements of Financial Statements of Business Enterprises, December 1980

FASB, FAS115, Accounting for Certain Investments in Debt and Equity Securities, 1993

Fine, A.E.M., et al, 'Proposals for the Statutory Basis of Valuation of the Liabilities of Linked Long-Term Insurance Business', Journal of the Institute of Actuaries, 115, 1988, pp 555-630

Flower, J., 'A Note on Capital and Income in the Law of Trusts ' in Edey, H. and Yamey, B.S. (eds.), Debits, Credits, Finance and Profits, Sweet & Maxwell, 1974

Franklin, P.J. and Woodhead, C., The UK Life Assurance Industry, Croom Helm, 1980

Fraser, A., 'Valuation of Widows' Funds Where There is Appreciation in Values of Investments', Transactions of the Faculty of Actuaries, 1944, pp 207-218

Goford, J., 'The Control Cycle: Financial Control of a Life Assurance Company', Journal of the Institute of Actuaries Students' Society, 1985, pp 99-114

Hall, L.G., Review of Howitt, H. (ed.), The History of the Institute of Chartered Accountants in England & Wales and its Founder Bodies, 1870-1965, in Journal of the Institute of Actuaries, 92, 1966, pp 365-7

Harte, G. and Macve, R., 'The Vehicle and General Insurance Company Ltd', in Taylor, P. and Turley, S. (eds.), Case Studies in Financial Reporting, Philip Allan, 1991, pp 346-360

Hicks, J.R., Value and Capital, 2nd. edn., Oxford: Clarendon Press, 1946

Horton, J. and Macve, R.H., 'The Development of Life Assurance Accounting and Regulation in the UK: Reflections on Recent Proposals for Accounting Change', Accounting, Business and Financial History, 4(2), 1994, pp 295-320

Horton, J. and Macve, R., Accounting Principles for Life Insurance: A True and Fair View?, ICAEW, 1995

IASC (International Accounting Standards Committee), Framework for the Preparation and Presentation of Financial Statements, 1989

ICAEW (Institute of Chartered Accountants in England & Wales), Implementation in the United Kingdom of the EC Council Directive on the Accounts of Insurance Undertakings, Technical Release: FRAG 33/92,

ICAEW, November,1992

Inland Revenue, The Taxation of Gilts and Bonds, A Consultative Document, May, 1995

Jellicoe, C., 'On the Methods Pursued in Valuing the Risks of Life Assurance Cos', Transactions of the Institute of Actuaries, I, 1849, pp 1-14

Jenkins Committee on Company Law: Memorandum of Evidence Submitted by the Council of the Institute, Journal of the Institute of Actuaries, 86, 1960, pp 215-220

Jenkins Committee on Company Law: Discussion, Journal of the Institute of Actuaries, 89, 1963, pp 105-124

Johnson, L. Todd and Reither, C.L., 'Viewpoints: Reporting Comprehensive Income', Financial Accounting Standards Board ('FASB'), Status Report No.270, November, 1995, pp 7-11.

Kaldor, N., 'The Concept of Income in Economic Theory' in An Expenditure Tax, Allen & Unwin, 1955, pp 54-78.

Lyon, C.S.S., 'The Financial Management of a With-Profit Long Term Fund: Some Questions of Disclosure', Journal of the Institute of Actuaries, 115, 1988, pp 349-404

Macve, R.H., `Inflation Accounting and the Accounts of Insurance Companies', a series of four articles in The Post Magazine and Insurance Monitor, Vol. cxxxvii, Nos.35-38, September, 1977, pp 2097-101, 2173-8, 2225-6, 2291-5

Macve, R.H., `The FASB's Conceptual Framework: Vision, Tool or Threat?, paper presented at the Arthur Young Professors' Roundtable at the Arden House campus of Columbia University, New York, 7 May, 1983

Macve, R.H., 'Accounting for Long-term Loans', in Carsberg, B. and Dev, S., External Financial Reporting, Prentice Hall, 1984, pp 90-108

Macve, R.H., 'Solomons's Guidelines: Where Do They Lead?', Accountancy, March 1989a, pp 20-21

Macve, R.H., 'Questioning the Wisdom of Solomons', Accountancy, April 1989b, pp 26-27

Macve, R.H. and Jackson J., Marking to Market: Accounting for Marketable Securities in the Financial Services Industry, ICAEW, 1991

Macve, R.H and Struyven, G.J-P.E, 'Influences on the Insurance Accounts Directive and its Implementation in the UK, France and Germany', a paper presented at the Ernst & Young International Accounting Symposium, University of Wales, Aberystwyth, 12-13 October 1995

Merton, R., `An Intertemporal Capital Asset Pricing Model', Econometrica, 41,5, September, 1973, pp 867-87

Needleman, P.D. & Westall, G., 'Demutualisation of a UK Mutual Life Insurance Company', Journal of the Institute of Actuaries, 118, 1991, pp 321-400

Paish, F.W., 'Capital Value and Income', Economica, November, 1940, pp 416-18, reprinted in Baxter, W.T. and Davidson, S. (eds.), Studies in Accounting, ICAEW, 1977, pp 179-81

Parker, P.W. & Gibbs, P.M.D., 'Accounting for Inflation: Recent Proposals and their Effects', Journal of the Institute of Actuaries, 101, 1974, pp 353-403

Pegler, J.B.H., `The Actuarial Principles of Investment', Journal of the Institute of Actuaries, 74, 1948, pp 179-211

Price Waterhouse, Budget Briefing 1995, Price Waterhouse, London, 28 November, 1995

Redington, F.M., 'Review of the Principles of Life Office Valuations', Journal of the Institute of Actuaries, 78, 1952, pp 286-340

Review of Lockhead, R.K., Valuation and Surplus, in Journal of the Institute of Actuaries, 63, 1932, pp 507ff.

SI1993 No.3246, The Companies Act 1985 (Insurance Companies Accounts) Regulations 1993, HMSO, December, 1993

Salmon, I.L. and Fine, A.E.M., 'Reflections on a Takeover of a United Kingdom Insurer: a Case Study', Journal of the Institute of Actuaries, 118, I, June, 1991, pp 59-170

Sandilands, F.E.P. (Chairman), Inflation Accounting, Report of the Inflation Accounting Committee, Cmnd 6225, HMSO, 1975

Scholey, J.K., 'Accounting for the Cost of Pension Plans', Journal of the Institute of Actuaries, 95, 1969, pp 393-444

Skerman, R., 'A Solvency Standard for Life Assurance Business', Journal of the Institute of Actuaries, 92, 1966, pp 75-84

Skerman, R., 'The Assessment and Distribution of Profits from Life Business', Journal of the Institute of Actuaries, 94, 1968, pp 53-100

Smart, I.C., 'Pricing and Profitability in a Life Office', Journal of the Institute of Actuaries, 104, 1977, pp 125-72

Smith, P.R., 'More Informative Disclosure of Life Office Affairs', Journal of the Institute of Actuaries, 99, 1973, pp 249-91

Solomons, D., Guidelines for Financial Reporting Standards, ICAEW, 1989

Suttie, T.R., `The Treatment of Appreciation or Depreciation in the Assets of a Life Assurance Fund', Journal of the Institute of Actuaries, 72, 1944-6, pp 203-28

White, R.E. & Holmes, B.T., 'The Effect of a Change in the Interest Rate on Life Assurance Premiums', Journal of the Institute of Actuaries, 70, 1939/40, pp 380ff.

Wright, P.W., `An Actuarial Perspective on the ABI SORP and Guidance Note on the Recognition of Shareholders' Life Profits' (paper presented at the Ernst & Young International Accounting Symposium, Aberystwyth, October, 1995), University of Wales, Aberystwyth Working Papers in Accounting and Finance, 1995

Zeff, S.A., 1978, `The Rise of Economic Consequences', Journal of Accountancy, December, 1978, pp 56-63

Zeff, S.A., `It's all right for real people to have theories too', Accountancy, May, 1996, p 97

Notes:

1. <u>Value and Capital</u> first appeared in 1939 and was revised in 1946.

2. So a footnote reconciliation of historical cost profits is required by FRS3. See also ASB (1995), 6.25.

3. The FASB is now undertaking a project on 'comprehensive income', in collaboration with ASB, which will <u>alia</u>, review this issue (Johnson and Reither, 1995).

4. Under FRS3 these revaluations gains on fixed asset investments would therefore be presented in STRGL recommended in the SORP for investment trusts (AITM, 1995).

5. The proposal originally applied to all taxpayers but, following widespread protest, will now not apply individuals, for whom the 'capital' returns from gilts will generally remain tax free (Ernst & Young, 1995, Waterhouse, 1995, p.12).

6. The accruals basis will usually be 'amortized-cost', although simpler approximations to the 'effective interest method to spread the premium/discount on acquisition over the period to maturity will be acceptable (Revenue, 1995, p.10).

7. The proposals were designed to facilitate the development of a market in 'stripped' securities (Bank of England 1995), a precondition for which is similar tax treatment of the coupon interest and redemption payments. will be treated as effectively a zero-coupon cash flow, the income on which will be the difference between initial cost and the amount received.

8. If valued on the amortized cost basis, note disclosure of both purchase price and current value is required 24(6)).

9. This is not a method recognised by FRS3 (ASB, 1993) or ED55 (ASC, 1990), both of which require any profit loss on disposal of an asset to be accounted for in the period in which the disposal occurs (e.g. FRS3, para However, pending the implementation of the Insurance Accounts Directive, the ASB amended FRS3 so that requirement, together with the requirement in para.13 that all gains and losses recognised for a period s appear either in P&L or STRGL (unless specifically permitted or required to be taken directly to reserve accounting standards or law), does not apply to insurance companies or insurance groups in respect of or losses on holding or disposal of investments (para.31A).

10. It does not apply to investments accounted for under the equity method, and investments in consol subsidiaries.

11. However, where there is a net disinvestment in a portfolio, a proportionate amount of the deferred gain losses should be written off to income immediately; and where it is determined that there has been an other temporary decline in the value of an entire portfolio, the value is to be written down and the loss charged a income of that period (CICA Handbook (1988), 4210.04-21).

12. As Mark Tippett has reminded us, Hick's income theory gave only an essentially intuitive treatment of the i of uncertainty on consumption and investment decisions and on income measurement through his <u>ex a</u> <u>ex post</u> analysis of 'expected' and 'actual' income (which even on these terms Kaldor challenged, in the tra on Lindahl's analysis (Kaldor, 1955), as analysed e.g. by Bromwich, 1992, Chapter 4, as income measu At the time of <u>Value and Capital</u> economic analysis had hardly begun to grapple with the issues raised by e acknowledgement of uncertainty. However, since the early 1950s, a great increase in our understanding way uncertainty impacts on economic choices has developed. In utilising Hick's analysis, as is conventio exploring the economic underpinnings of the accountant's concept of income or 'profit' (e.g. Sandilands, it is important to remember that results based on 'certainty' models may need fundamental reappraisal modelling uncertainty (e.g. Merton, 1973). However, for the purposes of this paper, we are focusing on the of changes in the rate of interest and, as these may be anticipated or unanticipated, they apply, in Hick's t to both <u>ex ante</u> and <u>ex post</u> incomes.

13. i.e. apart from transactions with owners.

Once such a category of 'elements' is acknowledged, a rationale for this existence of credit and debit balance sheet balances for 'deferred income and expenses' in traditional transactions based accounting becomes available (c.f. Ernst & Young, 1996). However, it is argued below that this is a less satisfactory device for achieving articulation than the use of strict asset and liability definitions coupled with a category of 'non-income' equity changes.

Thus the ASB purports to view the balance sheet and P&L as expressing two dimensions of the same economic construct, whereas in practical affairs they may each reflect different aspects of business reality (rather as Hicks (1946) saw 'income' and 'capital value' as expressible each in terms of the other, whereas in practical affairs (as Paish (1940) argued) they may each reflect different attributes of economic welfare).

The discussion here of value changes does not extend to the particular issues that arise in a period of inflation, which are fully discussed by Baxter (1975 and 1984). (The features specific to insurance companies are discussed in Macve, 1977).

Those relating to borrowings are not further discussed here but are in most respects parallel to those for investments (Macve, 1984; Draper et al, 1993).

The recent Inland Revenue proposal to base taxation of gilts and bonds on the income/costs reported in company accounts would also be subject to this manipulation unless the 'marking to market' basis is used. On the other hand, although all disposal profits and losses will in future be taxed as income, this does not have the same conceptual significance as an accounting determination of whether or not gains and losses from changing interest rates are income (albeit that the practical significance may be much greater). For if an investor is taxed on the redemption gain resulting from an interest rate fall, his reinvestment at the lower rate will result in lower taxable income in future - the timing of tax payments will be altered but not the amount of the taxable base in the long run.

Unlike the previous draft of Chapter 4, Chapter 6 of the Exposure Draft of the Statement of Principles does not now propose that the distinction between P&L and STRGL should rest on whether or not a profit is realised (ASB, 1995, p.10). It is not apparent under the present proposal how it is made clear that depreciation of fixed assets would be a P&L charge (c.f. Ernst & Young, 1996, p.7; ASB, 1996, pp.26-9).

Subject to the legal difficulties referred to in section I above.

There would still be scope for earnings manipulation by transferring investments between categories, even though balance sheet manipulation would be eliminated.

Changes in risk are not discussed in the classic analyses of income discussed here (e.g. Hicks, 1946; Paish, 1940) nor in most discussions of accounting principles (e.g. Solomons, 1989). This gives rise to difficulties in dealing with provisions e.g. for 'self-insurance' (ASB 1995; c.f. Macve, 1989, Baxter, 1996, pp.173-4). However, it seems clear that, ceteris paribus, increased riskiness of a cash flow is equivalent to a reduction of the 'certainly equivalent' of the cash flow and the income effect is therefore similar (c.f. Macve, 1984; Horton & Macve, 1995, pp.121-2).

The revised view in ASB, 1995 p.10 that realisation does not provide a relevant criterion for reporting gains and losses in STRGL is consistent with the analyses of both Hicks and Paish as to the nature of 'income'. However, under the Companies Act unrealised gains are always excluded from P&L subject to the special provisions for the unrealised investment gains and losses of insurance companies. The definition of 'realised' is however itself a creature of accounting convention (e.g. Horton & Macve, 1995, p.45).

The traditional exclusion of all capital gains may historically, be viewed as resulting from the historical development of investment accounting (where fixed-interest stocks preceded equities) so that it is understandable that, given the ambiguity of the nature of the changes in value of fixed-interest investments which result mainly from changes in the rate of interest (c.f. note 27 below) the convention that was originally chosen (and then later extended to equity investments) was not to recognise 'income' from such changes in value (a principle enunciated over a hundred years ago in Verner v. General and Commercial Investment Trust 1894), (2 Ch.239) and reflected in the special rules about distributable profits for 'investment companies' in CA 1985, sections 265-7). Flower (1974, p.86) suggests alternatively that the 'capital' and 'income' from bonds was originally distinguished in accordance with the lawyers' traditional res principle: 'a rise or fall in the market value

of the bond did not change the physical character of the bond; it was not therefore regarded as an elem⟨
income'.

25. Short-term fixed-interest securities may be a special case (Macve and Jackson, 1991, Chapter 1).

26. Parallel treatment should be accorded to redemption of fixed interest debt (c.f. Macve, 1984). Currently
requires gains or losses on redemption to go to P&L, but if the Draft Statement of Principles is adopted th⟨
basis for determining allocation between STRGL and P&L will presumably require corresponding chan⟨
FRS3 (Ernst & Young, 1996).

27. In the case of gilts ('riskless' securities) all changes are interest rate changes. In the case of corporat⟨
securities there may be a change in the interest rate reflecting a change in perception of risk of defau⟨
Macve, 1984). As Mark Tippet has pointed out to us, given the influence of e.g. managerial preferenc⟨
decisions as to the structure of the firm's activities, changes in the portfolio of investments held may be r⟨
signals of the extent of risk changes perceived by managers. We do not discuss here the wider macro-eco⟨
question of the interrelationship between levels of interest rates and anticipated productivity and ⟨
investment in the economy generally (c.f. Kaldor, 1995).

28. If investments are continually revalued all gains and losses will be 'unrealised' revaluations and taken to S⟨
and there will be no further gain or loss on disposal.

29. We do not discuss here the more recent development of 'unit-linked' life insurance, where the investme⟨
and return are borne entirely by the policyholder (e.g. Goford, 1985).

30. Reddington (1952), in discussing how to determine the necessary terms of fixed-interest investments to p⟨
'immunization' against interest rate changes, points out the conflict between these two objectives.

31. British actuaries have now accepted disclosure of market values of investments (as required for the pub⟨
annual returns of insurance companies to the DTI) but, as was argued for in the very first volume
Transactions of the Institute of Actuaries (Jellicoe, 1849, p.7; c.f. Review, 1932, p.507), still retain a conse⟨
approach to valuation of liabilities which may permit the effective continuation of hidden reserves (Ho⟨
Macve, 1995). By contrast, German insurers have continued to resist the publication of investment r⟨
values, as will in future be required by the EU Insurance Accounts Directive (Macve & Struyven, 1995).

32. e.g. Pegler, 1948, p.192. More recently, in interview with the authors in September 1992 a former Presid⟨
the Institute of Actuaries has stated: 'I don't think actuaries have cared about the accounts, never thought⟨
them. That's something the accountants do. What the accountants did in the published accounts was
immaterial to anything I did'. The rare exception has been when accountants have addressed areas s⟨
pension accounting (e.g. Scholey, 1969 reviewing APB Opinion No.8).

33. The BAJ incorporates as its predecessors both the JIA and the Transactions of the Faculty of Actuaries⟨

34. This was the basis of the Council's evidence to the Jenkins Committee (1960); see also Cohen Comm⟨
Discussion, 1947; c.f. Macve & Jackson, 1991, pp.11-17.

35. In actuarial terminology 'reserves' include both 'provisions' and 'reserves' as defined in the Companies⟨

36. The articles cited here are culled from an examination by the authors of the JIA from its inception t⟨
(including its original incarnation as the Transactions of the Institute of Actuaries (1849-52) and its incorp⟨
into the British Actuarial Journal from 1995). A similar systematic search of the Transactions of the Fac⟨
Actuaries has not been made, but similar examples may be found e.g. Fraser (1944) asks how far to take
for appreciating investment values (allowing for the fall in the valuation rate of interest)(p.208): 'The actual
of appreciation on a fund varies according to circumstances. Where a fund is young and annual additi⟨
the investments are large, appreciation is a disadvantage owing to decreasing interest return; where a f⟨
old and the assets are tending to decrease appreciation may be a direct advantage'. Similarly, in the disc⟨
of Anderson (1944), Haynes and Kirton comment (p.165-7) on how to 'immunize' the existing contracts (s⟨
bonuses can be maintained) while the next generation will get lower bonuses now interest rates have fall⟨
their view there is no justification for reducing the bonuses on existing policies if the rise in investment ⟨
is greater than the increase in reserves needed (at the new rate of interest), leaving bonuses unchanged. ⟨

comments are referred to by Redington, 1952, but are regarded as controversial in Perks's discussion of Redington's paper at pp.324-6).

47. In the course of this discussion Benjamin cited with approval Edey's (1963) argument that for any typical ordinary trading company 'the concept of an actuarial valuation could not be avoided', contrasting this with his own experience of auditing practitioners whose 'point of view was that an objective measurement of profit could be made on a purely retrospective basis'. In concluding the discussion on Bangert's paper, however, Corby (p.167) observed that, while actuaries needed to understand more about accounts and about 'true and fair' annual accounts were a different matter from a valuation made for a purchase of a company.

48. Parker & Gibbs (1974) categorise insurance companies as 'a side issue in inflation accounting' (c.f. Macve, 1977).

49. Some property investment companies have argued that the requirements of FRS3 (ASB, 1993) make 'a mockery of their reported figures'.

50. Even though it will facilitate the consolidation of the US GAAP results of US subsidiaries it is perhaps unlikely that many life companies will wish to do this for UK investments, as additional work may be needed to revalue some actuarial liabilities (for example those in respect of immediate annuity business) to reflect the revised yields on this basis, as distinct from the market value approach required in the DTI returns (Wright, 1995, 4.8-4.9). The recent changes in the taxation of UK gilts etc. discussed above may however change the balance of costs and benefits in favour of the amortized cost basis.

. This could also be a justification for spreading gains and losses on other forms of investment, e.g. equities, although, as it is virtually impossible objectively to segregate the influence of changing interest rates from other features, or to identify 'long-term' and 'short-term' investments, any 'spreading' would have to be done by some agreed convention (Horton & Macve, 1995, Appendix XIII). As noted above, at present, however, agreement has not been forthcoming on this aspect of the proposed SORP on insurers' accounting (ABI, 1995). Some of those arguing for spreading also do so on the basis that it is necessary to counteract the short-term volatility of market prices, of which the long-term trend takes time to emerge clearly. However, as this view essentially regards the current market price as not reflecting the best estimate of future prices, we would not ourselves rely on this argument, although we recognise that there is a variety of views among investment experts as to the degree of 'efficiency' of the stock-market (see further, Horton & Macve, 1995, Appendix XIII, pp.248-51).

. Legally, the revaluation reserve could presumably be used for this purpose (c.f. Horton & Macve, 1995, Appendix XIII, pp.256-9).

. The precise entries would be similar to those in Baxter, 1984, pp.161, 166-7 and Edwards and Bell, 1961, pp.204-7.

. We do not consider here the general issue of 'split depreciation' whereby the realisation of revaluation gains arising from other causes would also be fed back into P&L from STRGL, the entries again being similar to those in fn.43.

. Further consideration would also be needed for intangibles whose value is determined by their future earning power rather than their market price (namely 'replacement cost'), e.g. Baxter, 1975, p.137; c.f. Baxter, 1994, p.135.

. See e.g. the discussion in the accounts of the Prudential Corporation plc for 1995.

. The more modern and theoretically based 'balance sheet' approach (e.g. Solomons, 1989) to the preparation of financial statements is primarily driven by the use of the balance sheet changes as a means for calculation periodic profit, rather than by any theory of 'financial position' as such (Macve, 1983; 1989). Nevertheless it has had considerable influence (in combination with the prohibition in the Companies Act 1985, in turn derived from the EC Fourth Directive, against 'netting off' of assets and liabilities) in changing the structure of balance sheets, albeit without any coherent underlying theory of companies' risk structure (Macve & Jackson, 1991).

OPPORTUNITY COST REVISITED

Michael Bromwich

Opportunity Cost Revisited

Probably most people think of Professor Baxter as a researcher and commentator on financial accounting writing from a strong economic income and valuation perspective. In contrast, this paper reviews two of the relatively few articles written by Baxter explicitly in the cost and management accounting areas and considers their relevance to current teaching and to some strands of current research. These articles are 'A Note on the Allocation of Oncosts Between Departments' (1938) and 'Costing and Pricing: The Cost Accountant versus the Economist' (1961). Of course, these articles only represent a little of the thinking of Baxter and his LSE colleagues (both accountants and economists) in the management accounting area over the period 1935 to 1965. Generally, it can be said that they saw the same general economic framework being applied to accounting problems of all types. Financial accounting and management accounting were therefore seen at least in part through the same lens. Ideally, it was felt that information which was seen as useful to enterprise management should also be useful to shareholders and investors. However, in teaching substantially more time was spent on financial accounting than management accounting at least up to the mid 1960's.

Generally, this perspective embodied what we now call economic income and economic valuation, with a strong reliance on opportunity cost reasoning as exemplified in the ideas of deprival value. Interestingly, it is the latter strand that has figured more in the LSE publications over recent years. However, all these themes can be seen in Baxter's work. The dual use of this reasoning is exemplified in his book Depreciation (1971) which is equally valuable to management accountants and financial accountants.

Although the two articles to be reviewed here are more in the opportunity cost tradition, the economic income approach meant that even at a relatively early time, problems of the timing and uncertainty of cashflows and of profits were never far from the minds of writers in this tradition.

These articles of Baxters are of interest in at least two ways. They give a reminder of the importance of the opportunity cost logic and anticipate some contemporary research and practical problems. The note on the allocation of "oncosts" (now, perhaps, more confusingly called overheads) represents the use of opportunity cost reasoning at the height of the development of this school of thought and at a time when its intellectual foundations in economic theory were fully understood. These foundations indicate there is far more to the opportunity cost doctrine than now presented in the standard text book treatments, where the use of opportunity cost is restricted to simplified choices between decision alternatives and to tackling scarcity internal to the enterprise. The costing and pricing article (1961) used this framework in order to generate several ideas which anticipate many of today's concerns including the proxy measurement of opportunity costs (Zimmerman, 1979) and taking prices from the market as suggested by target costing.

Opportunity Cost Reasoning

It may be a good time to readdress the idea of opportunity cost. Perusal of a number of standard textbooks suggest that the concept itself is often worth little more than a couple of paragraphs in often some 1,000 pages. The concept seems to be presented usually as one of a list of cost concepts useful, generally, in one-off decision making between alternatives (for example, to use spare capacity or not). Some books say the concept is important, but do not say why, though internal scarcity and measuring the cost of foregone options are mentioned. The concept has been reduced to a piece of jargon that says something like the opportunity cost of a given action is the foregone benefits (usually expressed in terms of foregone net revenue) of the best rejected alternative.

The contribution of opportunity cost reasoning goes far beyond this. At the time Baxter was writing in the 1930's, this reasoning derived automatically from modelling rational profit maximising decision making in a perfect and complete market and served to portray the role of costs in such a market. It is important to realise the full strength of the logic behind opportunity cost reasoning because the work of LSE scholars in the 1930's sought to use this reasoning in a pragmatic way, in seeking to improve accounting in decision making using relatively simple examples and, therefore, did not make explicit the theory being used. Whereas, opportunity cost theory gives us a way of approaching many accounting problems and suggesting solutions in accordance with economic theory. Such solutions may often be at variance with traditional practices and throw doubts on such practices.

A fundamental idea behind opportunity cost reasoning is that of economic equilibrium. In a perfectly functioning market in full equilibrium, the alternatives selected by decision makers will be those which equate perceived subjective marginal benefits with marginal costs similarly defined. Prices in such a market will be common to all and, in equilibrium, will portray the marginal benefits foreseen from outputs by consumers and the marginal costs of the sacrificed outputs which otherwise could have been made with available inputs. The factor prices bid by profit maximising firms thus depend on the expected returns from the final good to be made by these factors, which depend on what consumers are willing to pay. The price that has to be paid for employed factors must be therefore greater than the marginal value products of these factors in their best alternative uses, which reflect the lower valuation put on these rejected outputs by consumers. Thus factor prices taken from the market reflect foregone alternatives and in this sense all costs used by economists are opportunity costs. This analysis is really just another way of stating the well known marginal conditions for an economic welfare optimum where no further gains from trade can be made. Thus the full rigour of economic equilibrium can be said to attach to opportunity cost. This reasoning can also be shown to apply in multi-period decision making and under uncertainty with regard to state contingent outcomes.

In earlier parts of the period being considered, this theory was used to seek major changes in conduct. For example, with this reasoning, it can be shown that the familiar injunction to public enterprises to seek to make marginal cost equal to price is fundamentally flawed when applied to non-market settings. The advocates of this theory anticipated several modern problems such as the need to take risk attitudes into account in decision making under uncertainty (though how to do this was not apparent at the time) and the difficulty of monitoring decisions under opportunity cost reasoning. This latter view, perhaps, derived from a strong LSE heritage which sought to place accounting within the general sphere of business administration. For example, de Paula in a letter to the Director on his resignation as part time professor in 1929 wrote..... "it does not seem to me that Accounting should be taught as a separate technique but that it should form part of business administration so that the student may appreciate the place of Accounting in the organisation of a business, its functions and uses to Management". This concern with monitoring may explain many of the difficulties being experienced by those researchers in the agency and contracting areas who seek incentive structures based on ex post results which encourage efficient decision making in the sense of achieving goal congruency with the principal. In non market situations, factor costs may not measure in any real sense the opportunity cost of past decisions and therefore may not comprise an element of a rational reward structure that ensures efficient decision making. This perspective may explain some of the difficulties encountered by those seeking some simple incentive function based on say residual income. In a non-market setting or an imperfect market, the cost side of such measures obtained using traditional accounting cannot measure the opportunity costs of rejected alternatives to accepted projects.

An important contemporary issue, the role of accounting in internal and external contracting and the transaction costs relating thereto was examined in some detail by Thirlby in the 1940's and 1950's (see Buchanan and Thirlby, 1973). As a final example of the early use of opportunity cost reasoning, Edwards used this to present almost the classical definition of the value of private information as it is now understood 'unless the information supplied enables management to do something or refrain from doing something its collection is a nonbusiness proposition' (1937, pp.88).

Opportunity cost provides a good understanding of both costs from an economic perspective and of their role in resource allocation when taken together with the ideas that decision making should encompass only costs and revenues which vary with changes in activity (incremental and marginal costs and revenues). Thus, opportunity cost reasoning combined with a focus on relevant and incremental costs gives a powerful apparatus derived from a general economic model, for seeking to understand costs especially in complex situations. Opportunity cost reasoning thus provides the theory which supports and is intertwined with such concepts such as incremental cost, avoidable cost and sunk cost.

Some of the generally agreed foundations of opportunity cost reasoning are that:

(i)   Decision making is about the future. We can only regret the past and try to minimise such future regrets by efficient decision making.

(ii)   The costs involved are therefore of necessity subjective (as are all other valuations in economics), and personal. Here, cost is the perceived benefits of the rejected options and has meaning only at the time of choice and, therefore, different opportunity costs may accrue with plans of differing lengths.

(iii)   The cost of any decision is the best foregone alternative which, once rejected, can never be enjoyed. The fruits of any rejected alternative may not be able to be measured in any way ex post.

(iv)   The cost of any foregone alternative is subjective and borne by the decision maker and therefore cannot be measured by others.

(v)   What matters for decision making is the variations between alternatives.

In two important articles Gould (1962 and 1971), made the point that seeking to use opportunity cost explicitly in decision making is redundant. A view that was not received with unalloyed pleasure by Coase (1990, p.9 and p.11). In order to quantify opportunity costs, it is necessary to know the value of the alternatives being considered. It is therefore more parsimonious to use such values directly in decision making as they are the primitives of the decision problem. Certainly, the force of this argument comes across in looking at the simple opportunity cost problems in any management accounting text book, which are generally amenable to simple solutions without reference to the opportunity costs of decision options. Such a use of opportunity costs may add only confusion where student understanding of opportunity cost reasoning is doubtful. Gould's argument can, perhaps, be best appreciated by considering the derivation of shadow prices in a linear programming model. Here, to obtain shadow prices you need to solve the primal problem which also provides an optimal solution. Thus, shadow prices are redundant for the original decision.

In the light of this argument the suggestion was made by Solomons that opportunity cost should be taken to refer to the best alternative outside the set being considered. So in comparisons of options, opportunity costs will be used to value items which could otherwise be used in the best rejected plan outside the set being considered. This role for opportunity cost is subscribed to by Horngren, Foster and Datar (1994), who illustrate the use of opportunity cost reasoning being restricted, but opportunity costs associated with the opportunities arising outside these options comprising part of the costs of the considered options (1994, pp.338-339). This approach to avoiding Gould's argument is presented in a specially thoughtful way in a recent influential book by Demski (1994, pp.264-269). Here, he sees opportunity cost referring to the best among the choices not considered. Thus, 'Opportunity cost is the best alternative foregone among those alternatives not explicitly searched' (p.266) and 'Opportunity cost is used to control for those options not considered' (p.266). This I think was not the original usage of the concept. Certainly, a number of examples from the LSE School suggest that the term opportunity cost could be applied to the best foregone alternative in the decision set being considered. Coase, in a retrospective article (1990), seems not to object to Gould's implicit use of opportunity cost in this way.

In any case, it is not clear how defining opportunity cost as applying to the best option outside the decision set being entertained saves the concept from Gould's criticism. Strictly to arrive at opportunity cost of the best 'non considered' alternative, its worthwhileness relative to all other plans not in the decision set has to be assessed. Again, the correct decision can be made directly without consideration of opportunity cost.

Even with Gould's criticisms, opportunity costs have a number of important direct uses. They can be used for decisions which do not change the basis of the original decision and they can be used for delegating or decomposing elements of the original decision to areas of the firm. A familiar example is using shadow prices derived from mathematical programme models to charge for 'overheads' to ensure that the use of the resources represented by overheads cover their opportunity costs in a decentralised firm. Opportunity costs may also serve as attention directors signalling the existence of constraints within the decision set and the benefits from relieving them at the margin. They also figure strongly in providing economic meaning to shadow prices in current articles on agency, contracting and the analysis of cost structures. More importantly, as Gould said, this type of criticism does not detract from the role of opportunity cost reasoning as providing an important framework for thinking about costs in complex settings from an economic perspective well grounded in economic theory.

Generally, with writers in the 1930's, this framework role of opportunity cost remained implicit. They wished to make the cost of individual inputs reflect their economic cost in the face of constraints on their uses, widely defined. Each cost item should be charged to a decision option on the basis of its opportunity cost if used in its already agreed next best use.

With this background which serves to remind us of the importance attached to opportunity cost by writers in the LSE school, we turn to considering two articles by Baxter in the LSE tradition.

Baxter On Opportunity Cost

This article contains a now familiar example of a departmental store which for some reason figures strongly in this literature. Coase (1938) also illustrates his arguments with a departmental store (pp. 137-141) and in a compliment to Professor Baxter says... 'some of the practices of the cost accountant, particularly those connected with the allocation of what is termed "oncost", seem open to criticism. I need not give any examples in view of the very able article by Professor Baxter who..... examined the problem of the allocation of rent in a department store and showed current practice to be misleading' (p. 136-137). In fact, later in the article he is not so inhibited.

162

Baxters article considers a store with 3 departments with some costs that can be traced directly to the various departments. Rent is allocated on the basis of departmental space and office salaries are allocated on the proportion of sales in each department. Departments B and C are shown to make losses using traditional accounting. The space they occupy could be sublet to two other companies without harming Department A. The solution as to how the accountant should inform the directors of the company is a very clearly presented version of the now familiar method of comparing incremental costs and revenues. The example must be one of the first suggested uses of the contribution approach in decision making, contribution is, however, labelled 'surplus yieided by each department'. These surpluses are calculated excluding expenses applicable to the business as a whole. This approach does not figure so clearly in the work of Coase and Edwards. Baxter's approach is to calculate the contribution of each department and all three departments are shown to make a surplus over their traceable cost. Deducting the rent from subletting (now, perhaps, franchising) the space of departments B & C shows that the surplus from one is less than promised by the best foregone alternative, renting it out. Coase's rather siinilar example indicates that this approach will not work when there are economies of scope (see Coase, 1938, pp. 137-141).

Baxter uses reasoning of a type he ascribes to Edwards who uses incremental and marginal reasoning to criticise the arbitrary allocation overheads in costing and pricing. The reasoning utilised is that departments should be retained providing they cover their prime cost and any avoidable costs attaching to them and, of course, that there are no more worthwhile options for the resources being used. This suggests to Baxter that allocation of overheads should not be included in cost statements used for:

(i)   Decisions to continue or shut departments.

(ii)   To determine whether the departments are avoiding unnecessary waste. Here allocation is seen as pointless because managers have no control over general expenses.

(iii)   In the pricing of individual goods. Here sales prices should be set to maximise profit and not with reference to an averaged cost figure, '... a "cost" which can be varied enormously by altering the method of calculation (e.g, by allocating rent in proportion to cubic space instead of area) can not be regarding as specially sacrosanct' (p.270).

Baxter is one of the first commentators in this area to point out the paradox that although bad decisions flowing from using fully allocated costs should be reflected in reductions in profits, successful companies continue to use this approach without evident damage. The same statement can be made today. Survey after survey have indicated that overhead allocation is used extensively though these surveys generally seem to be addressed to the use of formal accounting systems. Little research has been undertaken on how firms approach non-routine, one-off decisions. It might be suspected that it is here that incremental cost and opportunity cost reasoning reign (probably without the dignifying titles) otherwise it is difficult to see how companies survive in a strongly competitive market.

Baxter allows that traditional costing has clear advantages which may offset the disadvantage of not using incremental costing. He cites many non-controversial benefits of the traditional approach and also argues that successful costing requires a through understanding of the economic ways of organising the firm's activities. Thus, he gives an example of the introduction of a full cost costing system requiring a complete reorganisation of a business including, among other things, 'buying coal with a higher calorific value, smoothing of floors to prevent breakages, the remedying of staff grievances concerning salaries....' (pp. 271-272). Similarly, many contemporary studies of, for example, the introduction of activity costing, record improvements to operating systems being associated with this operation. However, it is difficult to believe that costing or management accounting systems (of the traditional sort) encourage continual attempts to improve operations, in a way that continually, and fully, compensates for the misleading signals generated by such costing systems.

One of Baxter's approaches to reconciling this paradox seems to be original and uses opportunity cost reasoning. Thus, allocated rent may remind managers that utilised or underused space may have opportunity costs in terms of foregone uses of that space. Thus, while the general manager's salary might not be reduced if department Z were given up, he would then have more freetime to improve the working of other departments or to start fresh departments; and the profits from his new activities might roughly equal the part of his salary that is allocated to Z (p.273). This is a theme returned to in the other research to be reviewed here. Baxter, thus argues first, that allocations of fixed costs may serve to remind managers that fixed resources have opportunity costs and secondly, that allocated costs may yield some proxy of the possible opportunity costs of the present uses of resources, although any such signal is, however, likely to be inaccurate. Baxter does, however, counsel that accountants ought not to rely on this possibility, but should try to estimate the opportunity costs when working out the possible results of a change in policy' (p.273).

True to the LSE school of thought he recognises that opportunity cost represents 'one of the biggest "costs" of performing any operation which involves no book keeping entry and so is apt to be overlooked' (p.272). This inability to capture opportunity costs in accounting systems may be one explanation of why surveys of such systems do not document the use of opportunity cost reasoning. It may also help to explain the reduction of time spent on textbooks on explaining the use of opportunity costs in decision making because they generally focus on the formal cost accounting system which often is integrated with the financial accounting system and generally adopts the same accounting principles. In his conclusions he says, in an important contribution, that costing calculations should be based on prime cost, ignoring overheads, but that prime costs should be widely defined and might include an allowance for incremental overheads. He also stresses in a very modern way that the margin over costs should reflect and be dominated by market considerations. Similarly, he argues that only costs that can be traced to departments and those reflecting the avoidable costs caused by a department's existence should be charged to departments and that overheads should not be departmentalised.

This article is a classical example of the incremental costing approach with a flavour of opportunity costing, variants of which have been taught in at least most UK universities over the years.

It should not be thought that those members of the LSE school of thought writing in the 1930's obtained any real acceptance of their ideas at the time. The professional journals in which some of these ideas appeared received influential critical letters. For example, Bigg, an important textbook writer, made the criticism, germane to Baxter and Coase's reasoning concerning departmental stores, that 'One of the great advantages to be derived from cost accounts is the explanation which they afford of the financial results disclosed by the normal profit and loss account' (see Solomons 1952, p. 136). A more extraordinary example of this type of criticism was that of Rowland (also a well known textbook writer), the senior accounting teacher at LSE at this time. Among other things, in the Accountant he compared Edward's ideas to Dr Johnson's leg of mutton "ill bred, ill fed, ill killed and ill drest" and in a letter to the Accountant he said he regarded these ideas "as dangerous nonsense made the more dangerous by a fog of words in which assumptions are disguised as truths". The criticised ideas mainly focused on incremental and marginal cost analysis. What he might have said if he had been addressing opportunity cost can only be imagined.

Opportunity Reasoning and Overheads

Writing 41 years later after Baxter, Zimmerman (1979) entirely independently of Baxter's article (1938) provides strong analytical support for at least part of Baxter's argument. He argues in a way echoing Baxter that where one has an indirect cost which is hard to measure allocation may proxy for this. Here what is in mind is a resource which has a fixed cost and which is liable to congestion problems or service degradation with increased use. Managers will seek to use that amount of the service which is optimal from their own perspective even though because of congestion this may impose negative externalities on other potential users. Personnel services or general computer systems may provide examples.

Zimmerman's clearest example is that of a contract that provides a given quantity of long distance telephone calls in return for a lump sum payment. Without some type of charging system, managers will use this facility as if it were free, even though their usage may create queues or cause others to use the more expensive conventional telephone system. The essence of Zimmerman's argument is the assumption that the demand for the service in mind is related in some way to a direct cost. Hiring more labour may, for example, impose additional burdens on the personnel department. It is shown that any allocation of service costs based on the usage of the factor which drives the service costs will ensure more optimal decisions in terms of resource allocation than where no system of charging for services is made. Managers in their decisions will thus take into account the cost of the service when considering decisions involving the service. This analysis provides strong support for allocation in relation to degradable services - such as Baxter had in mind - with regard to his discussion of the general manager and department $\underline{Z}$.

The necessary assumptions are strong and include that there is some relation between the usage and the costs to be allocated and that there is no other charging system which more closely captures the relationship between the service costs and service usages. If such allocations were to be used for other decisions, such as pricing, they may well be misleading because these allocations do not capture the underlying cost function of the service in any precise way. In some cases there are few problems with using allocated costs to remind managers of possibly foregone opportunities. If, for example, the space in department store could be either used by the store or rented out for a known rental (say the going market price per square metre for the area of the department store). Departmental managers could be charged this opportunity cost rental for their space as is the practice in many service industries. This would serve to remind them of the foregone opportunity and help to give them an incentive to cover this cost from net revenues or by economising on space usage or reducing other costs. There are dangers with regard to cost reduction. Freed space may not be of a sufficient size to rent to others and other costs may be reduced below their optimal level.

More generally, it is not obvious whether costs can serve the role of proxying for foregone opportunities. For example, what cost could proxy for opportunities foregone by salesmen or for the use of non-congested capacity. Generally, in a non-rigorous way, this approach will work only if some constraint on resources exists, and optimal use of this resource to maximise revenues at the margin of its use is known, or can be estimated. These are the conditions for deriving a shadow price from an optimisation model. Otherwise, an allocation per unit may distort decisions away from the short run profit maximising optimum because these figures may be used in decision making as if they were costs variable with production volume. To avoid this problem, overhead charges seeking to remind managers of foregone opportunities need to be neutral with respect to decision making (say a fixed lump sum charge). Baxter has thus set researchers a challenge to which they have yet been unable to come up with a full satisfactory solution. The second article by Baxter to be reviewed here suggests one solution to this problem.

Baxter on Opportunity Costs in Budgeting

We now move on 23 years and consider briefly the article 'Approaches to Pricing: Economist versus Accountant' (1961) authored by Baxter and Oxenfeldt (a professor of marketing). The earlier part of the article makes the classical contrast between the extremes of the accountant's approach to pricing problems using cost-plus pricing and the economist's use of incremental and relevant costing based on opportunity cost reasoning. The now well known problems of cost-plus pricing are indicated very clearly. Three concerns are especially worth noting.

The first is the problems arising from jointness which make allocation arbitrary and subject to debate. The correct approach to joint assets is one which still causes controversy. Contemporary suggestions include the use of market prices and transfer prices based on willingness to pay, the setting of charges above incremental cost but at or below stand alone cost, and charging these costs to the organisational unit in organisational or product hierarchy at which these costs become avoidable if the unit is shut down. An alternative approach is to levy some decision neutral tax in order to recoup the net revenue expected from such joint costs at the time of the decision to acquire them.

The second concern mentioned in the article is the ignorance of displaced alternatives in cost - plus exercises. Here Baxter seems to be subscribing to the full blown theory of opportunity cost as associated with LSE and exemplified by the work of Coase (1938). Baxter argues that "cost can be measured realistically only by taking into account the alternative opportunities open to the firm. To find the sacrifices that result from the decision to do a job (the economist argues), logically we must look only to the period that still lies in the future at the decision date, and must estimate the changes in future expenses and revenues that result from the decision, a procedure that obliges us also to estimate what these expenses and revenues would be if the job is not done" (p.294). Baxter defines opportunity cost for his purposes as net revenue foregone on the acceptance of a job rather than its best alternative.

The third problem is how should the margin in cost-plus pricing be set. Baxter accepts the argument that where a firm has numerous products it cannot, on a routine basis, resort to the demand and costing studies ideally required by his 'straw man' economist. He accepts that demand is difficult to estimate and says that the accountant's pricing system is cheap to operate and, importantly, allows delegation.

The budgeting process is considered in order to help reconcile the differences between the economist's and the accountant's views of pricing. The budget summarises the firm's plans and expectations in terms of relatively long run expected profit and generates an expected or planned average costing margin per unit of each product class. This margin can be regarded as a price per unit in the sense that is, 'a charge, say, per man hour, for the service of converting direct materials into finished goods...... The price quoted for a job can therefore be regarded as avoidable cost plus a processing charge reflecting the net revenue foregone from using the resource on this product rather than its next best alternative. The argument is that the costing margin should be regarded as implied allowance for opportunity cost, and other things. The budget exercise produces a planned or expected contribution per unit of a product which when sold at budgeted volumes, at least, covers the benefits from the next best alternative product of a product class excluded from the budget plan, and, if achieved, ensures that budget decisions are realised. Thus, in routine pricing, maximising subject to avoidable costs and a margin (which indicates what was expected to be obtained from this product class) seeks to ensure that the price is sufficient to cover the foregone net revenue resulting from the production of that product class, as determined in the budget. With this view 'the traditional costing margin - overheads plus profit - may serve as a rough guide to opportunity cost' (p.302). Profit maximisation is considered at budget time and routine pricing decisions are made using a technique which seeks to ensure that these decisions are consistent with the budget.

Baxter accepts this is, perhaps, an unusual view of costs but now it may be seen as one which has some commonality with aspects of 'target costing' as it is said to be practised in Japan. Both approaches emphasise the importance of the market in pricing. With these views, as far as possible, prices should be taken from the market. Both approaches also seek to achieve a target set by management, often a market share or return on sales in Japan and a desired profit under Baxter's scheme. The two approaches differ in how the target is to be used. In target pricing, costs are to be reduced if they are otherwise expected to exceed the market determined price less the management's target. Baxter's approach emphasises the dominance of the market at budget time and uses budget plans to obtain a managerial target which is seen as a charge above direct costs which should be covered if plans are to be achieved.

The idea of target costing with its emphasis on the market was received with considerable shock by many contemporary Western managements in the 1980's. The ideas in the Baxter's article are therefore likely to have been seen as far more shocking and even further removed from practice in the 1960's. Baxter anticipates this and other difficulties with costing margin ideas but says that even when use of the firm's resources involve no added costs, these resources do 'represent the firm's opportunity to create net income and a cost must be placed upon them if the firm has alternatives' (p. 305). Thus, he sees the costing margin as a crude and imperfect tool but the least objectionable one available.

From a contemporary perspective, a number of questions arise. First under what conditions will the usual overhead allocation procedures proxy for a contribution margin. This possibility seems not unreasonable where output is restricted by resource constraints. Here allocation based on the scarce resource can be conceived as a proxy for the relevant shadow price. It seems less obvious that allocations can play this role where the opportunity cost derives from market conditions. Allocations based on resources cannot obviously 'shadow' demand conditions. Moreover, the usual reaction of managers to being charged costs is to seek to minimise them. In contrast, the aim of the costing

170

margin is guide the manager in the routine selection of projects, that is, the manager is meant to respond to the costing margin by seeking projects, the net revenue from which will cover this margin. Finally, there is the positive question of whether management do see overhead allocations in this way which as far as I know has not been investigated.

The two articles reviewed provide a very clear presentation of incremental and relevant costing and opportunity cost reasoning. They also seek to reconcile practical and research approaches in a way that informs practice. Re-reading these articles may suggest that opportunity cost reasoning plays a stronger role in decision making than is perhaps accorded to it by contemporary textbooks.

If nothing else, opportunity cost theory provides a general way of considering complex costing problems in comparisons of options, especially in association with incremental cost reasoning. As a possible example of this use of opportunity cost reasoning, I have no doubt that Professor Baxter's earlier studies of opportunity costs informed his later research on deprival values and their important role in accounting for price change.

References

W.T. Baxter, 'A Note on the Allocation of On Costs Between Departments', The Accountant 5, November, 1938, pp 633-636. Reprinted in D. Solomons (ed.), Studies in Costing, (Sweet and Maxwell), 1952, pp 267-276.

W.T. Baxter and A.R. Oxenfeldt, 'Costing and Pricing: the Cost Accountant versus the Economist', Business Horizons, Vol.4, No.4, Winter, 1961, pp 77-90. Reprinted in D. Solomons (ed.), Studies in Cost Analysis, (Sweet and Maxwell), 1968, pp 293-312.

J.M Buchanan and C.F. Thirlby (eds.), L.S.E. Essays on Cost, LSE, 1973.

R.H. Coase, 'Business Organisation and the Accountant', The Accountant, October - 17, December, 1938. Reprinted in D. Solomons (ed.), Studies in Costing, (Sweet and Maxwell), 1952, pp 105-158.

R. H. Coase, 'Accounting and the Theory of the Firm' Journal of Accounting and Economics 12, 1990, pp 3-13.

J.Demski, 'Managerial Uses of Accounting Information', Kluwer, 1994.

R.S. Edwards, 'The Rationale of Cost Accounting' in Sir Arnold Plant (ed.), Some Modern Business Problems, pp 277-299. Reprinted in D. Solomons (ed.), Studies in Costing, (Sweet and Maxwell), 1952, pp 87-104.

J. R. Gould, 'The Economist's Cost Concept and Business Problems' in W. T. Baxter and S. Davidson (eds.), Studies in Accounting, ICAEW, 1962, pp 141-155.

J. R. Gould, 'Opportunity Cost: The London Tradition', in H. Edey and B. S. Yamey (eds.), Debits, Credits, Finance and Profits, (Sweet and Maxwell), 1974, pp 91-107.

C.T. Horngren, G. Foster and S. Datar, Cost Accounting: A Managerial Emphasis, 8th edition, (Prentice Hall), Englewood Cliffs, N.J., 1994.

J. Zimmerman, 'The Costs and Benefits of Cost Allocation', Accounting Review, July, 1979, pp 504-521.

SCHMALENBACH, ZAPPA AND LIMPERG:

THREE "ACCOUNTING HEROES" OF CONTINENTAL EUROPE

John Flower

Introduction

In reflecting on the contribution that Will Baxter has made to the development of accounting as an academic subject, my mind went back to the 1994 Annual Congress of the European Accounting Association which was held in Venice. The rooms at the Zitelle Congress Centre where the various sessions were held, were named after important personalities in the history of accounting, notably:

- Limperg (Netherlands)
- Edwards (Great Britain)
- Zappa (Italy)
- Paton (USA)
- Skrzywan (Poland)
- Schmalenbach (Germany)
- Kimura (Japan)
- Saario (Finland)
- Cubillo (Spain)
- Savary (France)

At first I was rather indignant that Will Baxter had not been so honoured as I felt that his contribution certainly merited it, but then I realised that he lacked one essential qulification for inclusion in the list - he was still very much alive! However, as an Englishman, I was a little skeptical about the honour thus bestowed on R.S. Edwards, as I felt that his contribution to accounting had been rather oblique. Therefore on the first evening of the congress, I conducted a small sample survey. I asked my companions around the dinner table if they agreed with the choice of names for the meeting rooms. I do not claim that my investigation was very scientific : the sample of persons questioned was very small, not at all random and no doubt we were all very tired after a hard day's work at the congress. But the answers were very striking. Everyone agreed with me that, in the case of Great Britain, Edwards could not be considered the single outstanding personality in accounting; that there were several other persons with an equal claim. The same comments were made in respect of Paton (USA), Cubillo

(Spain), and Savary (France). In respect of Skrzywan and Kimura, my dinner companions, regrettably, had to admit complete agnosticism. Everyone had heard of Saario, but views on his importance were rather mixed. However in respect of the three remaining persons, there was complete agreement that they were the outstanding personalities not only in their respective countries but in continental Europe. I was intrigued by my companion's conviction on this point, because, although I was dimly aware of the names of Schmalenbach, Zappa, Limperg, I had no real idea of their significance in the development of accounting thought. I was rather appalled by my ignorance which was evidence of an intellectual divide between the Anglo-Americans on the one hand and the Continental Europeans on the other. This article is a small attempt to bridge this divide. It starts with a brief biographical sketch of each of our "accounting heroes".

Eugen Schmalenbach 1873–1955

Eugen Schmalenbach was Professor of Business Economics (Betriebswirtschaftslehre) at the University of Cologne from 1906 to 1933. Prior to being appointed a professor at the age of 33, he had had eight years' practical experience in business, firstly as an apprentice in an engineering works and then in his father's lock-smith business. Only at the age of 25 did he to college, to study economics and business at the Leipzig College of Commerce. His rise in the academic world was meteoric. Despite having only a diploma (acquired after only two years of study) rather than the full degree that was the norm, he was appointed an assistant at the nearby University of Leipzig. After three years he moved to Cologne, where he stayed for the rest of his life.

He retired from his position as Professor in 1933 at the age of 60. Almost certainly this action was provoked by the rise to power of the Nazis in that same year. Schmalenbach's wife was jewish and he showed very considerable personal character and courage in continuing to stand by her throughout the twelve years of "The Third Reich". Although he was obliged to adopt a low profile, this did not inhibit his activities as an author; in fact many of his major works stem from this period. The Nazis made use of many of his ideas for improving the efficiency of German industry; the most notable example was the

Reichskontenrahmen imposed by Hermann Goering in 1937 which was largely inspired by Schmalenbach's pioneering work on charts of accounts. However Schmalenbach can hardly be blamed for this. Only in the latter years of the war was he in any real danger, both from the bombings and from the Gestapo, and he was forced to go into hiding for a short period.

The principle that guided Schmalenbach throughout his career was the pursuit of efficiency, both at the macroeconomic level and within the business firm. According to Günther Sieben, who now occupies Schmalenbach's old chair at Cologne University, the postulate of efficiency was his "lodestar" (Potthoff and Sieben, 1994, p.82). Schmalenbach pursued this goal not only through his teaching and writing as a university professor but also in his activities as a business consultant and professional accountant. For thirty years, he owned a major interest in an auditing company which served as his window on the business world. He was the auditor of a large departmental store and frequently acted as consultant both for companies and for the government.

He was interested in efficiency as a means of improving the well-being of the whole of society. The contribution of the business firm to the welfare of the population was measured by the value of its output of goods and service. If the value of the outputs exceeded the value of the inputs consumed, then the firm would have made a positive contribution to the general welfare. Hence Schmalenbach was very interested in the measurement of profit, but more as a measure of the firm's efficiency from the viewpoint of society, than as a reward for shareholders or management.

The pursuit of efficiency is the common thread that runs through all his writings. He was a prolific author. He wrote more than a dozen major books and literally hundreds of articles and book reviews. Most of the latter appeared in the journal which he founded and which is still today one of the leading German academic publications under its present title of "Schmalenbachs Zeitschrift für betriebwirtschaftliche Forschung". A list of his major works is given in Table 1, which gives a general impression both of the quantity and the range of his output; subjects covered included the management of the economy, the organisation of the firm, finance, costing and pricing, charts of accounts and accounting principles.

Year of first Publication	Title	Translation
1915	Finanzierung	Methods of financing
1915	Die Aktiengesellschaft	The Limited Company
1919	Dynamische Bilanzen	Dynamic Accounting
1925	Kostenrechnung und Preispolitik	Cost accounting and pricing policy
1927	Der Kontenrahmen	Standard charts of accounts
1933	Kapital, Kredit und Zins in betriebswirtschaftlicher Beleuchtung	Capital, credit and interest for the fi
1941	Über die Dienstellengliederung im Grossbetriebe	Divisionalisation of large firms
1943	Gedanken eines Betriebswirtschaftlers zum Wiederaufbau zerstörter Grossstädte	Thoughts on the reconstruction of bombed cities
1943	Über die exacte Wirtschaftslenkung	Exact economic regulation
1944	Über die zukünftige Gestaltung der Betriebswirtschaftlehre	On the future of the science of busine administration
1944	Allgemeine Grundsätze ordnungsmässiger Bilanzierung	General principles of orderly accoun
1948	Pretiale Lenkung	Guiding through prices
1948	Die Optimale Geltungszahl	The optimal guide price
1949	Der freien Wirtschaft zum Gedächnis	In Memory of the Free Economy
1950	Die Doppelte Buchführung	Double-entry Book-keeping

During his lifetime, Schmalenbach was, far and away, the most celebrated academic accountant in Germany. For years he was chairman of the Association of Teachers of Business Economists and when he retired he was m honorary president. He was a conscientious and effective teacher. Certainly his teaching had a powerful and perma effect on his students, which ranged from utter devotion in the case of certain "disciples" to rejection on the part of th who were offended by his often strongly expressed views.

In the teaching area, Schmalenbach seems to have given most attention to the postgraduate course in auditing, w he set up in 1912, many of whose graduates were to become outstanding members of the profession, inclu Professors Walb, Mahlberg and Geldmacker. Even today, over 40 years after his death, Schmalenbach's influence on. For example, the Schmalenbach Society, originally formed in 1932 by a group of former students, is still the important research association in the field of business economics.

Schmalenbach's contribution to accounting thought

As demonstrated by the list of his major books in Table 1, Schmalenbach wrote very widely and contributed to the development of many topics in the field of accounting and finance. In a short paper it is impossible to deal with all these fields. Only the briefest mention can be made of his contribution to management accounting, notably the theory of internal pricing within the firm, by which individual decision-makers at all levels would be induced to take the right action from the viewpoint both of the firm and of society as a whole. He felt that if the proper value could be placed on every asset or activity (he referred to the "optimale Geltungszahl" or optimal guide price) much decision-making could be delegated to the lower levels of the organisation.

Dynamic Accounting

It is proposed to give a full account of only one aspect of Schmalenbach's work : his theory of dynamic accounting. This has been chosen because it is, probably, that part of his life-time output for which he is best known, both within Germany and outside, and also because it is also probably the least understood, at least outside Germany.

Schmalenbach used the term "dynamic" to describe his accounting to emphasise the difference from "static" accounting. Static accounting, which predominated in the late 19th century was based on the balance sheet which listed the assets and liabilities of the enterprise. Profit was calculated as the increase in net wealth reported in successive balance sheets. Under the static theory, profit was not only a secondary calculation; it was of secondary importance. Of primary importance were the values of assets and liabilities. Schmalenbach sought to change all this. He wanted to make the measurement of profit the principal function of accounting, for profit was the ultimate measure of the enterprise's efficiency. Hence he placed the emphasis on the measurement and reporting of costs and revenues, rather than of assets and liabilities.

Costs and revenues had to be distinguished from cash payments and receipts. Over the enterprise's entire life-span, profit may be measured as the difference between cash payments and receipts. Some academics, notably Riegen, argued that this was the only scientific measurement of profit. Schmalenbach was more pragmatic. He saw "the uselessness of obituary accounts that reviewed the life of the deceased". (D.A.R. Forrester, 1977. p.35). Hence a periodic measurement of profit is required, for a year, or, ideally, for a shorter period.

The period's cash receipts and payments are converted into the period's costs and revenues by setting up "buffer" or suspense" accounts in which, for example, a cash payment of the current period, which should be recognized as a cost of a future period is carried forward to that period. For Schmalenbach the balance sheet is nothing more than a collection of suspense accounts. In his book, "Dynamic Accounting", Schmalenbach presented a scheme for the dynamic sheet, which to this day is reproduced in every German introductory accounting text : it is shown in Table 2.

Table 2: Dynamic Balance Sheet

Activa	Passiva
1. <u>Cash</u>	1. <u>Capital</u>
2. <u>Payments, not yet expenses</u>	2. <u>Expenses, not yet payments</u>
e.g. i. purchased plant to be depreciated ii. prepaid rent	e.g. trade creditors
3. <u>Payments, not yet receipts</u>	3. <u>Receipts, not yet payments</u>
e.g. loans made	e.g. loans received
4. <u>Revenues, not yet expenses</u>	4. <u>Expenses not yet revenues</u>
e.g. self-made plant to be depreciated	e.g. provision for deferred maintenance
5. <u>Revenues, not yet receipts</u>	5. <u>Receipts not yet revenues</u>
e.g. i. trade debtors ii. finished goods	e.g. customer deposits received

Schmalenbach accepted that his dynamic balance sheet in no way measured the total wealth of the enterprise. He considered that it was impossible for one set of accounts to measure both profit and wealth. His approach is thus the complete opposite to that of Hicks, who regarded profit and wealth as necessarily linked, as it were two sides of the same coin, and which seems to dominate current thinking in Britain. For Schmalenbach the wealth of the enterprise could only be established by means of a separate calculation, in which the balance sheet played no direct role. He proposed that the value of the enterprise be calculated on the basis of the present value of future profits, estimated on the basis of reported past profits.

For Schmalenbach the most important quality of profit measurement was that it should facilitate comparability both between enterprises and between periods. It was more important that profit measurements should be comparable rather than absolutely correct. However Schmalenbach suspected that the enterprise's management could not be trusted to prepare accounts that were objectively comparable and that they would be tempted to manipulate the reported profit to their advantage. Hence he proposed that the measurement of profit be circumscribed by a number of accounting principles, whose principal function was to restrict the discretion of management to manipulate profit. The most important principle was historical cost. In his youth, Schmalenbach was attracted to the idea of reporting certain assets as realizable value (for example marketable securities held as speculations) but as he matured he forsook such frivolities and came more and more to insist on the primacy of historical cost. There appear to be two reasons for this attitude.

• He was strongly opposed to the practice of reporting fixed assets at current value, as had been permitted under German Commercial Law in the later 19th century. In Schmalenbach's view, certain companies had exploited this freedom to write up their fixed assets to quite unrealistic values and thereby to report essentially fictional profits. Furthermore the use of current values led to large fluctuations in the reported profits which were quite unrelated to the underlying performance of the enterprise.

- A second reason was that Schmalenbach was very concerned to ensure a "fair" allocation of costs between periods. He likened the successive accounting periods to persons and argued that the assets that are carried forward from one period to another should be valued in a way that is fair to both periods. It was important that one child should not be favoured at the expense of another. This concept inevitably leads to practice of allocating historical cost in a systematic fashion over successive accounting periods.

However, Schmalenbach qualified the historical cost principle with two other principles:

(a)   The realisation principle : assets should continue to be valued at historical cost until there is a change of ownership.

(b)   The "Niederwertprinzip" : principle of lower value. Current assets, particularly stocks, were to be valued at the lower of cost and market.

Modern commentators have severely criticised Schmalenbach on insisting on these principles. Coenenberg points out that, in certain circumstances, the application of the realisation principal leads to accounts being less comparable over time. For example in the case of a long-term contract, taking all the profit in the final year leads to that year being favoured in comparison with earlier years, so that the successive profits are in no way comparable. Also valuing inventory at lower market value leads to the costs of a future period being lightened at the expense of the current period. Schmalenbach seemed to be aware of these contradictions but his priority seems to have been above all to avoid large unexpected charges in future periods. He seems to have been far less concerned about large future credits. This probably reflects his distrust of management's ability to resist the temptation to manipulate the accounts. Hence his asymmetric view of human nature (management is more likely to overstate profits rather than understate profits) led him to favour the asymmetric accounting rule of the principle of lower value.

Gino Zappa spent the whole of his career within the Italian university system : first as a student under Professor Bellini at the University of Milan and then as an assistant to Professor Besta, the leading accounting academic of the day, at the University of Venice, where he was described as "brilliant" and a "top pupil" (Canziani 1994, p. 146). In 1921, at the age of 42, he succeeded Besta as professor.

His principal works are "Le valutazioni" (Valuation), 1910, "Il reddito" (Income), first published in 1920, but substantially revised in 1929, and "Tendenze nuove negli studi di ragioneria" (New trends in the study of accounting). The latter, being the text of the lecture that he gave at the start of the 1926-7 academic year, set out his proposals for the creation of a new academic subject : Economia Aziendale (Concern economics). Over the next fifty years, he and his disciples, known as the "Zappiani", developed this subject in great detail so that today, the subject has become an institution in Italian universities, with courses, departments and degrees in Economia Aziendale.

Non-Italians find difficulty in understanding what are the special features of Economia Aziendale that distinguish it from the science of business administration as taught at British and American universities. One source of their difficulty is that the Italians themselves cannot make up their mind. Thus Canzioni (op.cit. 1994) asks the question whether Economia Aziendale is to be defined by its methods (e.g. systematic approach) or is it to be referred to as a clear-cut defined field of study.

However there does seem to be agreement on a number of rather general points:

-       Economia Aziendale, in principle, covers all forms of economic organization at all levels: the household, the business firm, public enterprises, towns, up to the state. The word "azienda" is a generic term, often translated as "concern".

-       Economia Aziendale's aim is to develop the general principles that govern the equilibrium and development of the azienda as a coherent unity. Zan (Zan 1994) characterises Zappa's contribution as a "radical holistic approach" based on a "unitary view of the azienda". Hence in developing the appropriate accounting system for an azienda, all aspects of its management and activities have to be considered.

-     The approach is in no way normative. The aim is to analyse and understand the azienda. Canziani (op.cit p.150) suggests that Zappa's approach was "critical positivism". On the basis of judgement and deductive reasoning, the scientist selects certain hypotheses, which are then confirmed or refuted by scientific observations, which are of an essentially empirical character. The analysis of the results leads the researcher to correct or modify the original hypothesis. Zappa considered his approach to be a mixture of deductive and inductive reasoning.

Although Zappa's concept of the general science of Economia Aziendale seems, at least to the uninitiated, rather vague, thankfully his ideas on accounting are rather more concrete. Income was the most important phenomenon in the economy of the azienda and the principal function of the azienda's accounting system is to measure income. For income to be measured scientifically, it must be based on observable facts, that is exchanges between the azienda and the outside world. Economic values only enter the accounting system through the action of exchange with third parties. Costs and revenues are measured at their exchange value, that is the amount of money expended or received. The term "money" includes debtors and creditors. The income of the azienda can only be measured with certainty when all its activities have been liquidated into money, which generally occurs at the end of its life. The real phenomenon is the "total-life" income", which is a variable continually in the process of becoming. Periodic income is merely an accounting fiction, which is needed for running operation from a practical point of view (Zan, 1994, p.290). In order to measure periodic income, special account must be taken of activities that cover more than one period. Zappa makes a clear distinction between:

-     Primary measures: costs and revenues relating to activities where the exchanges both started and were completed within the period. These costs and revenues can be measured with certainty.

-       Secondary measures: Costs and revenues relating to operations for which the exchange either occurred in a prior period or will occur in a future period. Examples are the use of a machine that was originally bought in a prior period or the production of goods to be sold in a later period. By a process of calculation, which Zappa seems to regard as essentially artificial, these economic values of past and future periods are included in the economic production of the present period (Canziani, 1982, p.62).

Secondary measures are further subdivided into:

-       valori stimati (estimates), where it is possible that the economic value placed on the cost, may be confirmed in a future period - an example is the provision against doubtful debts.

-       valori congetturati (conjectures), where the cost represents a pure allocation on the part of the accountant. Typically valori congetturati cover more than two periods and there is no scientific way in which they can be divided between the intervening periods. Examples are the depreciation of fixed assets and the costs and revenues of long-term construction contracts. Since by their very nature, the valori congetturati allocated to the intervening periods cannot be measured scientifically, most periodic calculations of income are indeterminate.

Zappa's concept of the profit and loss account is presented in Table 3.

Table 3: Zappa's concept of the Profit and Loss Account

for period n

Initial work in progress (costs sustained up to n - 1) (secondary measures)	Revenues measured by monetary transaction (primary measures)
Costs measured by monetary transactions (primary measures)	Future revenues and final work in progress (costs for n + 1)(secondary measures)
Depreciation (secondary measures)	

In prescribing rules by which the values of secondary measures could be estimated, Zappa was confronted with the requirement that they should not conflict with the prescriptions of the civil law, which were based on the twin principles of continuity and 'certainty of rights', which seek to assure that similar cases are decided in a similar manner. In the field of accounting these qualities were achieved by the application of:

-    monetary magnitude for the primary measures, and
-    historical cost for the secondary measures, tempered by the prudence principle which implied the lower of cost and market.

Hence, in practice, Zappa accepted that non-monetary assets be valued at historical cost. His view of the balance sheet was that it was of secondary importance, its main function being as an instrument of income determination.

Finally as Zan points out (Zan, op.cit.p.291), the unitary nature of income makes it impossible to value individual assets or to calculate the economic contribution of any singular element in terms of partial results. One result is a preference for the all embracing T format Profit and Loss Account. In Zan's view this form of income statement "is the logical result, the internally consistent consequence, of the radical holistic approach which conceived income - even accepting the fiction of periodic income - as the global juxtaposition of revenues and costs, and which refuses to accept any reductionist view which splits the integrally coordinated system into partial subsystems made up of operations and their associated costs, revenues and margins".

Theodore Limperg 1879-1961

Apparently Theodore Limperg's career was divided into two contrasting halves: up to 1922 he was a successful professional accountant, being a partner in a major auditing firm; however in that year he resigned his partnership on being appointed Professor of Bedrijfseconomie at the University of

Amsterdam, a position which he held until his retirement in 1950. However this appearance of two radically different careers is deceiving. As a professional accountant, he was primarily interested in questions of principle. For example, in 1903, early in his career, he founded the journal Accountancy for which, as editor for over 20 years, he wrote numerous articles, in the fields of accounting and auditing. Similarly as a professor, he maintained a keen interest in business matters, particularly in auditing, serving as an advisor to his former firm. Throughout his career, both before and during his time as professor, Limperg played a leading role in the Dutch auditing profession. He qualified as an auditor in 1904 by passing the examinations of the NIVA (Nederlandsche Instituut van Accountants). However two years later he split with this body, apparently because he was dissatisfied with its standards and set up a rival body, the NAV (Nederlandsche Accountants Vereenigung). He was able to mould this body more according to his higher ideals; thus its examination system, its code of professional conduct and disciplinary boards all reflected his determination to raise the competence and the status of the auditor. In 1919, the two bodies merged, essentially on Limperg's terms. From then on until his retirement, Limperg continued to play a leading role in the affairs of the Dutch profession. It is generally regarded that the high reputation of the Dutch profession in terms of the competence and integrity of its members owes a great deal to Limperg's influence.

Limperg's works

Limperg was interested in a vast array of topics : cost accounting, theories of value and profit, finance, organization theory, theory of labour, and, above all, auditing. Yet he did not write a single book. What is known today of his ideas and theories comes from three sources:

i)   The recollections of his contemporaries, particularly students who attended his lectures at the University of Amsterdam. As Muis points out ""The expression is never "Limperg wrote", but "Limperg said"" (Muis, 1980, P.69).

ii)   His lecture notes which were published in seven volumes after his death.

iii)   Some 80 articles published in Dutch journals, notably Accountancy to which reference has already been made, and Maanblad voor Accountancy en Bedrijfshoushoudkinds which he founded in 1924 and which is still one of the leading Dutch journals. All of Limperg's written work was in Dutch.

It is proposed to cover in detail only two aspects of Limperg's works: his theory of auditing and his theory of value. They have been identified as those parts of Limperg's theories that made a major impact in the Netherlands (Camfferman and Zeff, 1995, P.117).

Limperg's theory of auditing

Limperg set out his theory of auditing in a series of lectures entitled "The Theory of Inspired Confidence". They were published in the Maanblad voor Accountancy en Bedrijfshuishoudkunde in 1932-3; in 1985 the Limperg Institute published an English translation under the title "The social responsibility of the auditor". Limperg's principal aim was to define rigorously the function of the auditor in society and in the economy. He considered that it was essential that the auditor be independent of the entity that he audited, that is independent both of the management and of the owners/shareholders. The auditor should not permit any limitations on the scope of his work. At that time it was common for auditors to contract limited audits of enterprises, the extent of their audit being set out in long and detailed audit reports. Limperg doubted whether the public in general understood the significance of these lengthy audit reports and proposed that the auditor's "report" should be limited simply to the auditor's signature on the accounts. If the auditor performed his task according to the high technical and moral standards demanded by Limperg, then he would add value to the accounts and perform a socially useful function. In effect, Limperg sought to elevate auditing from a private function governed by the contract between the auditor and the audited to a social function regulated in the public interest by the professional institute.

Bedrijfseconomie

Limperg's second great interest was the development of the science of bedrijfseconomie ("business economics"). He set out his aims in his inaugural lecture on being appointed professor at the University of Amsterdam in 1922. At that time, the only other university department of bedrijfseconomie was at Rotterdam. The professor at Rotterdam, J.G.C. Volmer, who, by a curious coincidence, had been the leading partner in the auditing firm that Limperg had joined at the start of his career, had developed bedrijfseconomie as an essentially pragmatic subject, in which practical business problems were solved by a mixture of common sense and ad hoc reasoning. Limperg rejected this approach; instead he sought to raise bedrijfseconomie to a science. He considered bedrijfseconomie to be a part of the wide science of economics and he took the basic aim of economics to be the maximisation of welfare whereby humankind's wants were met by the optimal utilisation of available resources. He called the force whereby man strives to satisfy his material needs the "economic motive".

According to Camffermann and Zeff (op.cit. p.116), this approach gave Limperg's theory of bedrijfseconomie its two salient characteristics.

i)   It was normative and deductive. It was unashamedly prescriptive in telling businessmen what they should do. It was strictly deductive, being based on the economic motive. Empirical research was never a characteristic of Limperg's work. "When practice was found to deviate from a properly deduced theoretical norm there had to be an error in practice".

ii)   The strict confinement of the theory to economic motive meant the it was limited to certain aspects of that enterprise's activities. Accounting in particular was central, as it measured the progress achieved in achieving economic aims. However, the basis of the firms accounting systems should be the science of economics and not the traditional art of the accountant. (Muis, 1980, p.69).

To guide the businessman in making correct decisions, Limperg developed a complex theory of economic values. As expounded by Camffermann and Zeff (Op.cit. pp. 118-119) this theory is virtually identical to the Anglo-American theory of "value to the owner" or "deprival value". The value of an asset to its owner (the "opbrengstwaarde" or yield) is the higher of the "direct" yield, which is gained by the sale of the asset itself on the market and the "indirect" yield, gained from the sale of the goods or services produced by the asset. However the replacement value ("vervangingswaarde") places an upper limit on value, since, if deprived of the asset, the owner could restore his former position by replacing it. Limperg developed a "law of continuity" by which market forces would normally induce firms to continue their operations and thus maintain the intricate economy wide network of production in specialised firms. Thus for Limperg, to value assets used at replacement value was not based merely on a hypothetical replacement but on a replacement made virtually mandatory by the "law of continuity". It would seem that Limperg developed his theory of value in the 1920's about a decade before similar ideas began to become current in Britain and America. Camffermann and Zeff (Op.cit. p. 117) consider that both developments took their starting point in Austrian economics, especially as formulated by von Böhm-Bawerk, and should probably be regarded as independent derivations of the latter's work. There is absolutely no evidence that theorists in Britain and America were aware of Limperg's work before their first exposition in an article in Abacus in 1966 (Mey, 1966 and Clarke, 1984).

Limperg applied his theory of value principally to costing and pricing decisions. His interest in financial statements (the balance sheet and the profit and loss account) appears to have been limited to their providing a basis for the dividend decision. In accordance with the law of continuity, only as much should be distributed as would leave intact the firm's ability to produce. Hence depreciation of fixed assets and cost of goods sold should be based on replacement values. In the balance sheet, assets should be valued at replacement value (or lower 'yield' value) in proportion to their remaining life.

However Limperg never developed a rigorously sound theory of financial reporting. For example he excluded holding gains from income, on the grounds that the firm had not fulfilled its economic function until it had passed on its output to the consumer or to the next firm in the productive chain. However all holding losses were to be deducted from income. This treatment was both asymmetric (holding losses were treated differently from holding gains) but also not consistent with his theory of value. In effect Limperg introduced a dual capital maintenance concept : both physical and nominal capital should be maintained. He offered no clear arguments for this position. It has been suggested that his experience of businessmen's behaviour led him to attach more value to conservatism than was justified by his theoretical framework (Camffermann and Zeff, 1995, p. 120). Another example of his inconsistency was his ambivalent attitude towards secret reserves: he accepted that they could distort the reporting of profit but also acknowledged that they might be of practical value in running a business. As late as 1946, he defended the inclusion of a clause in the Dutch Institute's code of professional conduct that allowed an auditor to give a clear report on a set of financial statements that contained secret reserves, provided that the profit had not been increased by undisclosed transfers.

Common Ground

There is no evidence that our three accounting heroes ever met or even corresponded. It is known that both Zappa and Limperg were acquainted with Schmalenbach's writings, but, given that Zappa wrote only in Italian and Limperg only in Dutch, it is highly probable that knowledge of their work was limited to their own countries. Hence it is quite remarkable to discover a considerable amount of common ground in their work.

The feature common to all three authors' work was the primacy given to the profit and loss account over the balance sheet, to income over wealth. Two reasons have been advanced for this preference:

- A common reaction to the price inflation that hit Europe during and just after the First World War and which rendered problematical the former approach to financial reporting based on the balance sheet (Canziani, 1994, p. 151).

- A common intellectual foundation in the Austrian school of economists of Carl Menger and Eugen von Böhm-Bawerk.

It is interesting to analyse the works and careers of our three heroes according to the three bilateral relationships:

- Schmalenbach : Limperg
- Schmalenbach : Zappa
- Zappa : Limperg

Schmalenbach : Limperg

The careers of these two men were very similar. Both were:

- qualified accountants who throughout their careers interested themselves in the actual practice of accounting;

- had considerable business experience before being appointed a professor (Schmalenbach 8 years; Limperg more than 20 years)

- had very limited formal academic education and were essentially self-taught and self-made men.

In addition both men were intensely interested in improving the efficiency of business. But, despite their similar backgrounds and aims, one finds very little common ground in the content of the accounting theories that they developed. The common ground is much more evident between, on the one hand, Schmalenbach and Zappa, and, on the other, Limperg and Zappa.

Schmalenbach : Zappa

Their accounting theories are virtually identical in the following respects:

- The profit and loss account consists of cash payments and receipts that, in part, originate in past or future periods, and which are allocated as costs and revenues to the current period.

- The balance sheet represents past and future cash payments and receipts that have yet to be allocated as costs and revenue.

- Historical cost is the proper basis for the valuation of assets.

- The T form of the profit and loss account is to be preferred to the columnar form.

There is no fundamental difference between Schmalenbach and Zappa in their conclusions relating to financial reporting, only in the path that they followed to reach them : Zappa was the brilliant theorist; Schmalenbach the pragmatic practitioner.

Limperg : Zappa

The careers of Limperg and Zappa could not have been more different : the one, the successful accountant with over 20 years experience in business, the other the quintessential professor with little practical experience. Yet both sought to create their own personal conception of the science of business administration. Their theories were, of course, quite different : Limperg's bedrijfseconomie was normative and deductive, based on the science of economics. Zappa's economia aziendale was in no sense normative and was based on a mixture of deductive and inductive reasoning. However they had two important points in common.

- Each was conceived as a single unitary theory that covered all aspects of the firm in a scientific, systematic fashion.
- Each was the personal construct of its founder, strongly marked by his personality

Both men's theories became institutionalised in a school of thought. However it would seem that both schools were very much dependent on the personality of their founder. They survived for only about a generation after their death. The "Amsterdam" school of bedrijfseconomie, founded by Limperg, no longer exists (Camffermann and Zeff, 1994, p.128). It Italy the term "economia aziendale" is still current, but the nature of the subject is questioned by the young generation of accounting academics, who did not know Zappa. (Canziani, 1994, p.163).

Concluding remarks

All three of our accounting heroes were charismatic personalities who strongly influenced their contemporaries. However their influence has waned with the years that have passed since their deaths. Possibly time has been least kind to the two, Zappa and Limperg, who claimed that they had discovered the single correct approach to accounting. Perhaps it is the more pragmatic and practical approach of Schmalenbach that will be justified in the longer run. But all three have helped to mould the modern world and are worthy of our study.

References

(This list comprises only works in the English language. References to the authors' works in their original language may be found in Edwards, J.R. (1994)).

Canziani, A. (1982), "Measurements and Calculation in Accounting", Economia Aziendale 1 : 57-71

Canziani, A. (1994) "Gino Zappa, Accounting revolutionary", in J.R. Edwards (ed) Twentieth-Century Accounting Thinkers, London : Routledge

Camffermann K. and Zeff S.A. (1994) "The contributions of Theodore Limperg to Dutch Accounting" in J.R. Edwards (ed) Twentieth-Century Accountancy Thinkers. London, Routledge

Clarke, F.L. (1984) European Scholars, Bonbright et al, and Value to the Owner, Working Paper No. 14, University of Sydney Accounting Research Centre.

Edwards, J.R. (1994) Twentieth-Century Accounting Thinkers. London : Routledge

Forrester, D.A.R. (1977) Schmalenbach and After, Glasgow; Strathclyde Convergencies

Forrester, D.A.R. (1993) Eugen Schmalenbach and German Business Economics. New York : Garland

Galassi, G. (1984) "Accounting research in Italy" in A.G. Hopwood and H. Schreuder (eds) European Contributions to Accounting Research, Amsterdam : Free University Press

Klaasen J. and Schreuder H. "Accounting research in the Netherlands" in A.G. Hopwood and H. Schreuder (eds) European Contributions to Accounting Research, Amsterdam : Free University Press

Limperg, T. (1985) The Social responsibility of the auditor (English translation of articles published in 1932 and 1933), Amsterdam : Limperg Institute.

Mey, A. (1966) 'Theodore Limperg and his theory of values and costs' Abacus 2 : 3 - 23

Muis, J.W. (1980) 'Wie was Limperg?' Accountancy (UK) October 69-70.

Potthoff E. and Sieben G. (1994) "Eugen Schmalenbach" in J.R. Edwards (ed) Twentieth-Century Accounting Thinkers. London : Routledge

Schmalenbach, E. (1959) Dynamic Accounting (English translation of 1956 edition by K.S. Most and G.W. Murphy), London : Gee & Co.

Zan L. (1994), Toward a history of accounting histories. European Accounting Review. Vol. 3 no. 2

ON FORGING AN ACADEMIC ACCOUNTING COMMUNITY

Anthony G. Hopwood

The vitality of the British academic accounting community owes much to the pioneering endeavours of Will Baxter and his productive relationship with David Solomons. Together they provided the basis for an academic community based on ideas and the forging of understandings rather than one based on the serving of more immediate commercial interests. While in his inaugural lecture (Baxter, 1948, p.185) Will could aspire to "accounting ... becoming a worthy member of the academic syllabus", by his actions he and a small group of colleagues ensured that in the United Kingdom that aspiration became more of a reality.

That clearly was no mean achievement. The serious academic study of accounting has had to contend with doubters in both the academic and professional communities - and still does.

Within the academy, accounting has had an equivocal status. Whilst it is no longer necessary to engage in the explicit legitimizations of Henry Rand Hatfield (1924) appealing to the intellectual similarities between the double entry calculus and the more highly regarded mathematics, accounting research nevertheless has had to contend with the views of those normally of a curious disposition who have still accepted an unproblematic and professional view of accounting. Seeing it as mere technique and largely accepting the truth claims of the professional, many members of the wider academic community have adopted a stance towards accounting that they would not dream of adopting for law, medicine, engineering or many other areas of professional endeavour, although it has to be recognized that most of these areas also have had their own histories of struggle for acceptance in the world of ideas and debate. In the United Kingdom, Will Baxter and his colleagues at the London School of Economics laid the basis for changing the academic perception of accounting. Such a change would not be quick or easy, but by developing a direct research link between accounting and economics Baxter moved accounting inquiry nearer to being an appropriate component of the social sciences.

The relationship between the worlds of accounting practice and academic inquiry has been no less contentious. Upon his arrival at the London School of Economics Baxter would have been aware that there were already those who contrasted accounting reality with economic abstractions. In the years ahead he and David Solomons would become acutely conscious of the desire of many in professional practice to isolate professional education from the world of ideas and the emerging approaches stemming from accounting research (Zeff, 1996). A particularly forceful illustration of the gulf between the academy and the commercial world of accounting came with the absorption of the Incorporated Society of Accountants into the Institute of Chartered Accountants in England and Wales. The Society's tradition of encouraging the systematic study of accounting come to an abrupt halt, particularly significant being the termination of the journal Accounting Research which had provided a more scholarly outlet for the new economically oriented tradition of accounting inquiry. Any illusion that an easy and mutually agreeable relationship could be forged between the academy and the profession must have been shattered. Research was not to be a process of satisfying the needs for knowledge emerging from practice but rather a more fundamental process of attitudinal change. If accounting was to aspire to be a practice grounded on insight and understanding, then seemingly, its practitioners also needed to accept such a view. At the time most didn't and many still don't.

Throughout his career Will Baxter has accepted the difficulty of the task of constructing a more intelligent and thoughtful practice of accounting. He rightly has been suspicious of quick solutions. The immediacy of engagement with the accounting policy making process has been of less interest to him. Indeed he has been aware of the possible undesirable consequences of a more explicit policy arena in accounting, arguing that accounting education and research could suffer from too pronounced a concern with accounting standardization and specification (Baxter, 1962). Rather than wanting an immediate impact, Baxter had more faith in the value of a more conceptually grounded educational process and the slower encroachment of well thought out ideas.

Focusing thereby on developing a strong, thoughtful academic tradition committed to education and scholarly inquiry, Baxter laid the essential basis for what has become a productive and widely regarded

194

research community. Even within the sphere of professional practice, a significant number of British accounting academics have been called upon to play important roles in policy making and regulatory institutions. Indeed it would be possible to argue that British professional accounting has been poor at producing the statesmen who can mediate between professional practice and the institutions of the State. Requiring insights into accounting that go well beyond those implicit in the accounting calculus alone, many such roles have been filled by members of the academic accounting community.

Reflections on the Current Research Community

Having played such a formative role in the creation of an active academic community in the United Kingdom, Baxter also has commented on the consequences of his own creation. Invariably newly emergent communities develop a momentum of their own and usually have consequences very different from those implicit in their establishment. Will Baxter clearly thinks that this has been the case for accounting research and has made known his own unease with at least some current trends. In a bluntly worded commentary he reflected in the following terms (Baxter, 1988, p.19):

> "... academic accountants have taken the bit between their teeth and are moving far and fast from familiar ground. They seek to emulate the standards and ways of sister departments rather than the office. They find more stimulus in study of the abstract than of practice. They prefer pure to applied because pure comes more easily, is more fashionable and offers better career prospects".

With the passage of time I sense that such comments will be seen as far too polarized. Certainly they stem from a rather a historical view of the relationship between accounting research and practice. Will Baxter and others have had to contend with the critiques of practitioners who have attacked their own economic abstractions. And such critiques continue, as is evidenced by the current debates on the role that might be played by more basic formulations of accounting principles in the accounting standard setting process. David Tweedie, while striving to continue the intellectual traditions of Baxter, Solomons and other colleagues, is still seen by many practitioners as trying to import economic abstractions into a policy arena that should be guided more by the dictates of experience and custom and practice. And

195

at one level of analysis, they are correct. The income theoretic framework from which such principles emerge is indeed an abstraction from practice. Rather than providing an account of how accounting has become what it is and the form that it currently takes, income theory has focused on providing a normative framework for discussing what accounting might become. But that gap between the analysis of what is and the articulation of what might be is a question of legitimate concern and of very real potential interest to members of the academic community as well as conservative practitioners.

For like Baxter, I am not uncritical of some current developments in the academic community. One of my concerns is with the tendency to accept in far too static a form bodies of prevailing insights. I sense that unfortunately this has happened in the area of income theory. The earlier dynamics introduced by Edwards, Baxter and Solomons have seemingly been lost. Rather than seeking to take forward knowledge, too many have been concerned with merely applying it. Because of this I sense that it can still be argued that the knowledge remains in far too underdeveloped a state to enable easy application.

While Hicks' (1946) concept of income is still seen by many as providing a basis for the meaningful analysis of accounting measurement and valuation problems, much less consideration is now given to Hicks' own concerns about the complexities and utility of the income concept. Although Hicks laid the foundation for the systematic discussion of income measurement in a world of uncertainty, it could be argued that present understandings have advanced relatively little since then. Indeed all manner of other difficulties have entered the arena since that time as are so admirably summarized and discussed in Bromwich's Financial Reporting, Information and Capital Markets (1992). Diverse preferences, alternative sources of information and changing views of the functioning of investors and capital markets have all made discussions of income measurement more complex. The simple elegance of past understandings now receive less support and questions of the practical applicability of the resultant concepts are much more difficult to consider, let alone resolve.

If there also were to be a more systematic consideration of the implications of technological change for asset valuation and income measurement, uncertainties and even doubts could grow further.

196

Increasingly enterprises function in a world of dynamic change where there is little or no commitment to the performance of particular tasks. In such a world, notions of current value and potential replacement become much more difficult to answer and usually their resolution has little to do with accounting or even economic knowledges but more to do with the mobilisation of technological and wider understandings. In such a world, the value of the concept of income might become less obvious as commercial interest shifts to a more systematic analysis of the fund generating capabilities of enterprises and the incorporation of these insights into the wider bodies of knowledge with which modern markets function.

One could go on to review other ways in which the past understandings of accounting income have been challenged and made more complex. In many senses it seems a pity that the efforts devoted to the application of the simpler understandings of the past could not have been devoted to the exploration of the emerging uncertainties. But be that as it may, we nevertheless are left with a world where the immediate relevance of many earlier conceptual ideas becomes less and less obvious. What might have been considered applicable and relevant, is now increasingly seen as abstract and distanced from the complexities of practice. Increasingly it is as if there is a need for a more interdisciplinary research agenda that could provide a potential bridge between economic analytics and wider insights into the economic, commercial and technological functioning of both firms and markets.

The pragmatic need for such wider understandings of accounting has also become clearer as the regulation of accounts has become more significant and the domain of accounting policy making has come to encapsulate the world as a whole rather than the isolated nation state.

Modern accounting policy making is now confronted with the problem of making sense of international accounting diversity. Of course it is possible to interpret the differences in terms of either a differential distribution of ignorance or the outcome of a developmental process still in operation. If only the Germans would recognize truth or catch up with the more advanced development of the capital markets elsewhere, their accounting would be better! In the past it might have been possible to get away with such crude preconceptions. Now, however, it is recognized that accounting practices are enmeshed in wider institutional structures and bodies of thought. Even accounting within one country, such as the United Kingdom, can be under pressure to change if political structures shift and changes are perceived to be occurring in the balance of power within and around the enterprise (Burchell et al., 1985). There is now a much clearer recognition of the contingent nature of accounting practice, although at present the extent of our insights into the patterns of relationships between accounting and, for instance, structures of corporate governance, the modes of functioning of the state and the legal attribution of rights in the enterprise and its informational representation are all too minimally developed.

The same can be said of the understanding we have of both the institutions for and the processes of accounting regulation. The differential advantages of different regulatory structures are still inadequately explored. The accessibility of different approaches to regulation by different interest groups has not been investigated. We have little insight into the rationales behind the frequent capture of accounting regulatory institutions by the audit industry.

One could go on and on. But perhaps the most important point to make is that such insights and knowledge are important because wider institutions and pressures impinge directly on accounting. Because of them and through them, accounting is different than it otherwise would be. Indeed seen in such terms, accounting is not and cannot be detached from its context. It is not an isolated phenomenon properly amenable only to comparison with some detached and abstract indicator of its truth. Accounting is a much more pragmatic phenomenon than that, emerging and functioning within and shaped by the institutions of the modern commercial and socio-political world. Seen in such terms, a variety of different bodies of knowledge have an immediate relevance for both understanding and guiding the processes of accounting change and development. It is difficult, if not impossible, to hierarchically order knowedges in terms of their relevance to accounting practice, although if one were nevertheless to try to do so it is difficult to imagine that an abstract insight into the economics of income measurement could justify a place nearer to practice than an institutionally informed understanding of accounting regulation or a better appreciation of how shifts in the structures of corporate governance or modes of financing are likely to impinge on accounting.

Just as Baxter called for an interdisciplinary approach to accounting research in his inaugural lecture in 1947, so now such an outlook on accounting research is still relevant. Moreover, the reasons for it remain the same. For it would be difficult to improve on Baxter's formulation of the rationale in terms of the `how?', `why?' and `so what?' of accounting (Baxter, 1948, p.185). Noting that a challenging education in accounting needs to move beyond the mechanics of `how?', Baxter argued for a deeper insight into "the administrative and legal aims" that underlie the practice of accounting. Now we most likely would elaborate the description of the functional endeavours with which the practice of accounting has become intertwined, but we still would agree with Baxter that the subject needs to be understood in terms of its grounded institutional rationales rather than mere abstract conceptualizations. A study of the consequences of accounting as encapsulated by the `so what?' question is also as relevant as ever. Now, as then, the "power of making cool and detached criticisms" of the accounting craft is of crucial importance. Only through such means can accounting maintain the tension between what it is and what it might become that is so essential for ensuring the continued vitality of practice.

Discussion

Out of the small academic community established around Baxter and his colleagues has developed a large, questioning and productive accounting academy in the United Kingdom. Striving to understand both the factors that shape accounting as it is and the consequences that it has, increasingly accounting research has been based around a number of very different disciplines. Alongside the consideration of the economic logics implicit in accounting magnitudes, research now also probes into accounting's functioning in wider market processes and the ways in which the economic calculations which it offers emerge within and in part shape the functioning of quite complex institutional structures.

Increasingly I sense that it is not particularly productive to compare the relative practicality of different approaches. Not only is there inevitably a tension between them, such that each approach can provide its own very different insights into the functioning of the others, but also questions of relevance and practicality depend so much on the interpretative context and the problems under consideration. Research into the capital market utilization of accounting information could be highly relevant for discussions of the relative advantages of different ways of improving the information available to capital market users. Indeed it might sometimes suggest that there are valid alternatives to formal accounting disclosures. Equally, research into the relationship between forms of accounting and modes of corporate governance could certainly cast light on the contingent nature of technical practice but also provide insights into the accounting consequences of wider institutional changes. One could go on. However it is sufficient to state that a number of very different bodies of knowledge can claim quite legitimately to inform the processes of accounting choice, regulation and decision making.

Perhaps it is most important to note and indeed to celebrate that accounting knowledge is now on the verge of being able to address such issues. Accounting is no longer a subject that has to be addressed in terms of the customs and practice of its own technical functioning. Over the years accounting itself and the institutions for its propagation and regulation have become increasingly impregnated with ideas of its functioning and effects. Accounting is increasingly a subject that is difficult to disentangle from our ideas of it. Perhaps slowly and with some trepidation, accounting has started to enter a knowledge based age.

To a substantial degree, the activities of Will Baxter facilitated the process. He gave a considerable impetus to the processes by which accounting came to be examined, criticized and appraised. With other colleagues, he contributed to our ability to talk about accounting rather than merely to do it. And through such talk, accounting increasingly has been able to be associated with an ever wider array of policy issues, institutional arenas and intellectual concepts. That is a remarkable achievement.

References

Baxter, W.T., "Accounting as an Academic Study," The Accountant (6 March, 1948), pp.181-185.

Baxter, W.T., "Recommendations on Accounting Theory", in W.T. Baxter and S. Davidson, eds., Studies in Accounting Theory (Sweet & Maxwell, 1962), pp.414-427.

Baxter, William T., Accounting Research - Academic Trends versus Practical Needs (Edinburgh: Institute of Chartered Accountants of Scotland, 1988).

Bromwich, Michael, Financial Reporting, Information and Capital Markets (London: Pitman, 1992)

Burchell, S., Clubb, C., and Hopwood, A.G., "Accounting in its Social Context: a History of Value Added in the United Kingdom", Accounting, Organizations and Society (1985), pp.381-413.

Hatfield, Henry Rand, "An Historical Defense of Bookkeeping", The Journal of Accountancy (April 1924), Vol 37, No.4, pp.241-253. Reprinted in W.T. Baxter and S. Davidson, eds., Studies in Accounting Theory (London: Sweet & Maxwell, 1962), pp.1-13.

Hicks, J.R., Value and Capital: An Inquiry into Some Fundamental Principles of Economic Theory, 2nd ed. (Oxford: The Clarendon Press, 1946)

Zeff, Stephen A., "The Early Years of the Association of University Teachers of Accounting: 1947-1959", Working Paper, Rice University, 1996.

Printed in the United Kingdom by Bell and Bain Ltd., Glasgow